Prefix
MTW

0005897

KT-143-031

This book is to be returned on or before
the last date stamped below.

24 AUG 1998

14 JAN 2000

DISCARDED

Also available from Cassell:

Arlene Gorodensky: *Mum's the Word*

Richard Nelson-Jones: *You Can Help*

Richard Nelson-Jones: *Practical Counselling and Helping Skills* (4th edition)

THE DEPRESSED MOTHER

A Practical Guide to Treatment and Support

Kath James

LIBRARY
PEMBURY HOSPITAL
01892 823535

Cassell
Wellington House
125 Strand
London WC2R 0BB

PO Box 605
Herndon
VA 20172–0605

© Kath James 1998

All rights reserved. No part of this publication may be reproduced or transmitted in any form or by any means, electronic or mechanical including photocopying, recording or any information storage or retrieval system without prior permission in writing from the publisher.

British Library Cataloguing-in-Publication Data
A catalogue record for this book is available from the British Library

ISBN 0–304–33462–6 (hardback)
0–304–33463–4 (paperback)

9806144
WM 171

Typeset by BookEns Ltd, Royston, Herts.
Printed and bound in Great Britain by Biddles Ltd, Guildford and King's Lynn.

CONTENTS

Acknowledgements vi
Preface vii

1 An overview of depression in the community 1
2 What is depression? 7
3 Associated disorders 22
4 The increased risk of depressive illness in women 48
5 The disadvantaged mother 55
6 Postnatal depressive disorders 64
7 Postnatal depression and mother–infant relationships 76
8 Support for postnatal emotional well-being 81
9 Postnatal depression, relationships and men 95
10 Vulnerability to depression and the Edinburgh Postnatal Depression Scale 103
11 Why depression is missed 115
12 A multidisciplinary approach to detection and management 119
13 Stress 129
14 Maternal exhaustion 140
15 Physical treatment 146
16 Counselling 154
17 A new initiative: a self-report scale 163
Conclusion 167

Appendix 1 Resources and organizations 168
Appendix 2 Rating scales 172
Appendix 3 Leaflet: What's what on a question of sleep 174
Index 182

LIBRARY
PEMBURY HOSPITAL
01892 823535

ACKNOWLEDGEMENTS

I would like to thank: Dr Neil McQuire for his help on the sections in Chapter 3 relating to stress; Jean Ball and her publishers for allowing me to use material in Chapter 8 from her book *Reactions to Motherhood* (Books for Midwives Press, 1994), particularly Janet's story; and Dr Malcolm George for his article on postnatal depression and men, reprinted in Chapter 9.

I would also like to thank my husband Vic, for his patience, forbearance and encouragement over the last eighteen months, and my oldest friend, Denise, who never lost faith in me. Last and not least, a special thank you to my mum who never once complained when I neglected her because of my commitment to this book.

I very much appreciate the encouragement and editorial work of Cassell staff, particularly Marion Blake, Sarah Bury and Alison Hill, as the book was made ready for publication.

PREFACE

To look at a depressed woman who has just had a baby, is not simply to look at a depressed woman. She may be suffering from the consequences of pregnancy and the birth process, or perhaps the experience has allowed other feelings which have been locked away, waiting to emerge. She might have been depressed before she had the baby or she may be suffering from the consequences of the change in lifestyle, often unexpected and ill prepared for. She may be suffering from a postnatal depressive illness caused by the huge hormonal shift that she has undergone.

To understand and to help a person suffering from any illness is easier when the illness itself is understood. This is particularly so with any mental disorder, as greater understanding helps to allay fear. The removal of fear also helps the client to accept treatment and to recover more quickly, reducing the guilt which often accompanies mental illness. Relatives and friends will usually be able to cooperate in a more positive way if they understand the process that has caused the disturbance.

Depression is a journey; it has a beginning, a middle and an end. I hope that when you have read this book, you will feel able to join the mother and her family on their journey, and not just watch from a safe distance. To enable you to do this, I have explained depressive illness and many of its treatments through the spectrum, not just concentrating on postnatal depression as an entity in itself. I hope that this information will give you the confidence to use the skills that you have already acquired, and that any new knowledge gained will provide you with a sound basis from which to work.

In parts of the book you will see that I have asked you to discuss and question different aspects of the information which I have previously given to you. You can work alone to do this (for example in essay form), but, if possible, shared discussion is useful because so many of you will have different experiences to fall back upon and share with each other.

As you progress through the book, you will realize that I have talked about women and mothers generally, not placing emphasis on any special groups. I do realize that many ethnic groups have particular problems and sometimes different cultural approaches to mental health. I have not tried to explore this subject because it could possibly double the size of this book and there has already been much written on this topic. I hope that those of you with clients from minority ethnic groups will adapt my advice appropriately to the specific needs of your community.

Kath James
June 1997

1

AN OVERVIEW OF DEPRESSION IN THE COMMUNITY

THE ATTITUDES OF THE GENERAL PUBLIC

In December 1991 the Royal College of Psychiatrists in association with the Royal College of Practitioners conducted a survey, in conjunction with MORI, prior to the launch of the Defeat Depression campaign. The survey looked at the public's general perceptions of depressive disorders, particularly in relation to the causes, the stigma attached to depression and the misconceptions about its treatment. When the survey had been running for three years, it was repeated. This was to monitor any changes in people's attitudes. The main findings were as follows (MORI, 1995): Eighty per cent disagreed that 'depressed people were either mad or mentally unstable' – the same proportion as in 1991, but representing an increase (from 73 per cent to 79 per cent) in agreement with the statement: 'Depression is a medical condition like any other illness.' This showed that depression had become more acceptable as an illness in the eyes of the public. The proportion who strongly agreed that 'anyone can suffer from depression' had increased by 10 percentage points to 67 per cent. The proportion of men who said that they had had contact with depression, through suffering from it themselves or through a close family member or friend, had increased although women were still more likely to say that they had suffered from it themselves (27 per cent compared to 18 per cent of men). There was an increase, of 7 per cent, of those who disagreed that 'children are very unlikely to suffer from severe depression'. Nine out of ten people still agreed that people suffering from depression deserve more understanding and support from their family, and 92 per cent still favoured counselling as the main treatment for depression. Awareness of the cause of depression had increased considerably in every single case presented. People were aware that divorce and the end of relationships, postnatal depression and menopause/change of life can cause depression, and also cited redundancy, stress and physical illness as major causes. There was a fall of 7 per cent of those who thought that antidepressants are *very* addictive, although 39 per cent still mistakenly believed that they were. The proportion of people who thought that antidepressants were effective had increased by 5 per cent. There was still some confusion about the role of antidepressants in the treatment of depression, and about the difference between antidepressants and tranquilizers. There was still a reticence about seeking help, with 4 per cent of those interviewed saying that they would not seek help if they were suffering from depression. The GP was regarded as the main source of help for anyone suffering from depression, but there was some agreement that people with depression feel embarrassed to consult their GP.

DEPRESSION AND GENERAL PRACTICE

Each year 3 per cent of the general population are diagnosed by their GPs as suffering from depression and it is thought that another 3 per cent will be unrecognized on consultation (Goldberg and Huxley, 1980). Depression is managed mainly by GPs who will refer only about 10 per cent on for treatment by a psychiatrist. Of all patients consulting their own doctor, 5 per cent show major depression, another 5 per cent show milder episodes, and at least 10 per cent show at least some depressive symptoms. At least one patient with depression is likely to present at each surgery session (Williams and Skuse, 1988). Depression can occur at any age, but it occurs twice as frequently in women as in men, and particularly in women with babies and young children. (American Psychiatric Association, 1987).

Although GPs recognize and manage a large number of patients with depression, at any consultation at least half of the patients with depressive symptoms are not recognized. A further 10 per cent are recognized during later consultations, but 20 per cent may remain undiagnosed for at least six months (Goldberg and Huxley, 1980). The reason for failure to diagnose correctly may lie in the many different ways in which depression may present itself. The depression may have originated years ago and now appear to be part of the person's normal personality, or the patient may be slow to come forward with symptoms due to lack of insight or feelings of embarrassment (Freeling *et al.*, 1985). It is important that both the patient and the GP realize that being able to explain the depression in the light of recent stresses should not preclude it from specific treatment.

Of great importance also in the treating of depression in the community are the other team members who work with the GP. These are known as the primary health care team (PHCT) and include the practice nurse, the health visitors, the midwives and the district nurses. Other staff will include the practice manager and administrative staff, the receptionists and the attached service members who also belong to other teams. These may include the community psychiatric nurse (CPN) and a counsellor or psychologist who spends a set number of sessions each week with patients from a particular practice. If no psychologist is attached to the team, access to the psychology service at the local hospital is always available.

At one time it would have been taken for granted that within the PHCT all problems relating to mental health could be addressed by the CPN team specifically. However, due to external pressures it is becoming increasingly likely that other members of the PHCT will be called upon to provide support and counselling in cases such as postnatal depression and other non-psychotic depressive illness.

In 1994, the Secretary of State for Health commissioned a review of mental health (Department of Health, 1994). The resulting report provided a vision of how best to equip and deploy valuable mental health nursing to the best effect. It set out the future role of mental health nurses and their potential contribution in a wide variety of settings, as individual practitioners or as members of multidisciplinary and multi-agency care teams. It also provided a framework for action which would take into account policy developments, organizational changes and educational requirements in order to meet the changing needs of people for whom services are provided. The report drew attention to the community care initiatives which were resulting in the discharge of long-term residents with schizophrenia and other serious enduring mental illnesses into the care of the PHCTs.

The report drew attention to the importance of continued dialogue with GPs about care provision, especially given the number of developments in primary care led by GPs, nurses and health visitors. It pointed out that the skills of the mental health nurse should be an important resource for all members of the PHCT and should be directly accessible by the general public. Mental health nurses would need to collaborate with colleagues in primary care to create protocols which address the health needs of the local community. It is, however, possible to provide a broader framework for the particular work of the mental health nurses and their collaboration with the rest of the PHCT. Below is a suggested framework which would support the recommendation on page 16 of the report '... the essential focus of the work of mental health nurses lies in working with people with serious or enduring mental illness, in secondary and tertiary care, regardless of setting'.

Location of work	Purpose of work
Primary Prevention Reducing the incidence of mental illness. (People at risk approximately 250 per thousand per year) Needs the work of Health Visitors, District Nurses, School Nurses, Practice Nurses and the specialist support of Mental Health Nurses.	Work with vulnerable people or those at risk of mental illness
Secondary Prevention Early detection leading to prompt intervention. (People at risk approximately 100 per thousand per year) Needs the work of Health Visitors, District Nurses, School Nurses and Practice Nurses. Requires continuous liaison and some casework by Mental Health Nurses.	Early detection and case finding, leading to early intervention. Work mostly carried out in the Primary Health Care Setting
Tertiary Prevention Treatment and active intervention with established mental illness. (People at risk approximately 24 per thousand per year). Needs the work of Mental Health Nurses in hospitals, residential facilities, day and community care. Needs liaison and work with Health Visitors, District Nurses, School Nurses and Practice Nurses.	Early intervention effective treatment and rehabilitation requiring active case management

Source: *Mental Health Review*. Department of Health, 1994, p. 27.

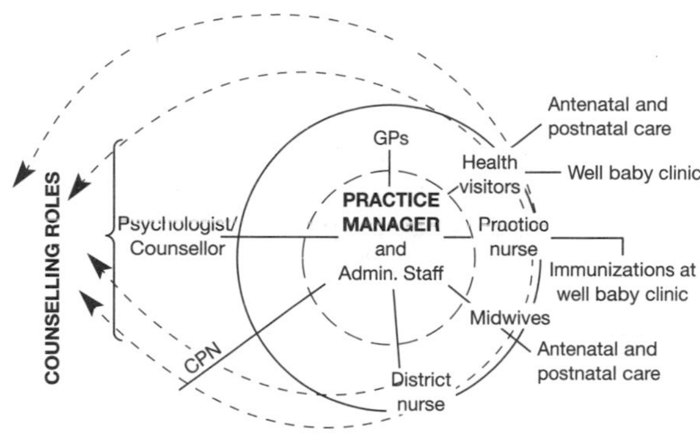

Figure 1.1 Points of contact between the PHCT and the mothers of young children

Figure 1.1 illustrates the points of contact with mothers of young children and the different members of the PHCT. As you will see, there are many areas that overlap and 'dovetail'.

- Which other groups may fit into the satellite circles?
- What is the role of the receptionist in the PHCT?
- Do the receptionists need some special training to enable them to approach and deal with depressed patients appropriately?
- What courses, appropriate to the subject of mental health, are available in your area?
- Discuss the term 'worried well'. Is there a term you find more appropriate? Consider the reasons for your answer.

REFERENCES

American Psychiatric Association (1987) *Statistical Manual of Mental Disorders* (3rd edn, revised). Washington: APA.

Department of Health (1994) Working in Partnership: A Collaborative Approach to Care. Report of the Mental Health Nursing Review Team. London: DoH.

Freeling, P., Roa, B.M., Paykel, E.S., Sireling, L.I. and Burton R.H. (1985) 'Unrecognised depression in general practice' *British Journal of Psychiatry* 290: 1880–3.

Goldberg, D. and Huxley, P. (1980) *Mental Illness in the Community: The Pathway to Psychiatric Care.* London: Tavistock.

Williams, P. and Skuse D. (1988) 'Depressive thoughts in general practice attenders', *Psychology of Medicine* 18: 469–75.

2

WHAT IS DEPRESSION?

Before looking into the depression which intrudes into the health of the mother, let us take a look at depression generally. Mild depression is a common emotional experience, but most people are able to cope with their feelings without letting them affect their daily lives. This statement puts depression into perspective. Many people will have one or more short, self-contained periods of depression during their lifetime, and emerge from them unscathed and possibly better for the experience. This is the type of experience that many of us will identify with. Many other people will have a long-standing, sometimes recurring depressive disorder that will never allow them to fulfil their full potential. Nothing will ever feel as good as it should do and their general quality of life will be undermined. These people appear to be functioning normally and are the group that is often missed. A more serious manifestation of depressive disorder occurs in the individual who can no longer function normally due to the constant intrusion of both mental and physical symptoms. In every sense of the term, this is depressive illness.

Much research has been carried out regarding the causes of depressive disturbance. This includes the various theories produced by psychoanalysts and psychologists, the traditional and new medical models and psycho/social theories. The latter will be discussed in more detail when the reasons for postnatal depression are explored later. Much work has been done in this area and I have extracted that which is relevant to the subject of this book – maternal depression – and that which is closely connected to vulnerability factors. Most of this will be better understood once readers have come to a global understanding of depressive illness *per se*. A discussion of the psychosocial causes of depression in other societal groups such as unemployed men and elderly people is beyond the remit of this book. For further reading, however, I recommend Brown and Harris's *Social Origins of Depression* (1987).

THE MEDICAL MODEL OF DEPRESSIVE DISORDERS

People who trained some time ago will be very familiar with the traditional classifications of the 'depressions'. However, *The British Journal of Psychiatry* (Hirshfeld, 1994) have produced a supplement that deals exhaustively with new classifications. These are based on the fact that no substantive evidence has been produced to prove that major and minor depressive illnesses are not actually part of the same disorder with the same group of causes. It will be useful for you to become familiar with both the new and the old definitions because other professionals, depending on when they trained and the level of their professional updating, may not always be used to both.

Traditional classification

Exogenous depression is caused by circumstances that come from without. This is a neurotic condition, as opposed to a psychotic condition, because the individual usually has clear insight into the causes. It is important to clarify the difference between exogenous depression and a normal grief reaction because it is normal to become depressed after the loss of a loved one or a precious belonging. It is when the reaction is prolonged or inappropriately severe that the condition becomes open to question.

A grief reaction is a disturbance in mood that is normal and necessary in an individual's life experience. It is the reaction to a real loss, and this may be tangible or intangible. In the early stages grief may be incapacitating, but as the acute initial reaction wears off this will not be so. A grief reaction is usually self-limiting and diminishes over the course of about a year. Hence people who have suffered a bereavement will often state that 'things got better' after the first complete set of yearly anniversaries (birthdays, wedding anniversaries, Christmas, date of death or separation, etc). In elderly people the process may take longer.

There are three phases of grieving:

- Shock and disbelief.
- A developing awareness of the pain of loss as the numbness wears off, which eventually results in crying. It is thought to be important that this stage should not be interfered with by the 'holding back of tears' – a fact long acknowledged by the wise people of this world!
- Restitution. The eventual elevation of the loved one or object to a degree of perfection. New objects replace the lost one at the end of this phase.

Exogenous depression is related to grief but it is not the same, in that it is a disturbance in mood that is a pathological reaction to a loss which may be actual, threatened, or imagined, and may be tangible or intangible. The resulting depression does not enter the stage of restitution within weeks or months, and is severe, prolonged and increasingly incapacitating in all areas of the individual's life. Although, if left long enough, many depressions may be self-resolving, professional help is often required if the individual is to regain any quality of life within a reasonable time. Exogenous depression is generally through to be less serious than endogenous depression because a trigger factor can be identified and the individual has the clear insight into the problem, as previously mentioned. Indeed, it is important to reassure the person because she will know that her reaction is not normal and may fear that she is 'going mad'.

Endogenous depression is thought to be caused by factors *within* the individual. In severe endogenous depression, psychotic features are often present and can take the form of delusions and/or hallucinations. *Delusions* are false beliefs, out of keeping with the individual's level of knowledge and cultural group; the belief is maintained against logical argument and despite objective evidence to the contrary. The delusions present in depression are often nihilistic, for example the patient may think that she cannot eat because she has no bowels. Individuals may have delusions of worthlessness and guilt. The patient may think that she is going to die because she thinks she has an illness such as cancer, or because she knows that she is going to die on a certain date. She may also display an unrealistic, intrusive fear of death, etc. *Hallucinations* are false sensory perceptions in the absence of an actual external stimulus. Any one of the five senses can be involved but the most common one is auditory. For example, the individual may hear voices stating that she is dirty and that she is a vile person.

People suffering from endogenous depression are likely to suffer from *diurnal variation of mood*: they feel worse in the morning and improve as the day goes on. They wake early, as opposed to those suffering from exogenous depression, who tend to have trouble getting off to sleep and do not want to wake up in the morning. However, Brown and Harris (1978) noted that one-fifth of patients suffering from exogenous depression also experience early morning wakening. As opposed to feeling better as the day goes on, people suffering from exogenous depression feel worse, although they can be temporarily lifted from their condition by good company, etc. Those individuals suffering from endogenous depression cannot be 'jollied' out of it, even temporarily.

New classifications

Major depression, according to the World Health Organisation (1992), requires five or more specific criteria for diagnosis, one of which must be depressed mood or loss of interest. The others are significant weight loss or gain, anhedonia, disturbed sleep pattern, psychomotor agitation or retardation, fatigue, feelings of worthlessness, a diminished ability to think, difficulty in concentrating and suicidal thoughts. The American Psychiatric Association (1987) stipulates also that the symptoms must have been present for at least two weeks.

Dysthymia replaces the concept of depressive neurosis and other mild chronic depressions. It must be present for at least two years and is a chronic, less severe depression, often with an insidious onset. The symptoms, which overlap with those of major depression, include guilt, loss of interest and difficulty in concentration. Other feelings, not seen in the classification of major depression, are pessimism, low self-esteem, lack of energy, irritability and decreased productivity.

Minor depression has symptoms comparable with those of major depression but only two of them need be present for diagnosis. This definition is a variant of less severe depression and the mood must be present for at least two weeks.

Intermittent depression is similar to minor depression with symptoms that are not constant. A depressed mood may last from a few hours to more than a week, and two additional symptoms of minor depression (four in all) must also be present. The illness must have lasted for at least two years for diagnosis to be made.

Recurrent brief depression is a full-blown depression which last from a few hours to a few days. The individual must experience a dysphoric mood or loss of interest, and exhibit at least four of the following symptoms: poor appetite, sleep problems, agitation, loss of interest, fatigue, feelings of worthlessness, difficulty in concentrating and suicidal thoughts and/or actions. One or two episodes per month for at least one year are characteristic of this form of depression.

- When looking at the classifications of depression, it would seem that the majority of the population would be able to identify with at least one of the descriptions at some time during their lives. If you are working in a group, how many of you thought 'that's me!' at some point during this chapter?
- Do you think that it is probably the time factor which is different for most of us? That is, do you think that most people suffer from some of these conditions at some time in their lives, but that the duration is shorter for 'non-depressive' individuals?

CAUSES OF DEPRESSION

Four of the major theories are psychoanalytical, cognitive, learned reinforcement and biological.

Psychoanalytical theory

From a psychoanalytical viewpoint depression is interpreted as a reaction to loss. For example, when a loss occurs in childhood, such as the loss of parental affection, certain feelings will surround that situation. When a new loss occurs later in life, the individual may regress to her original state when the earlier loss of perceived loss took place. This makes the person feel helpless and over-dependent on others. She continually craves affection and security and will internalize anger in order to receive it.

Much of Freud's work was related to depression following the death or loss of a loved one. He also concentrated on the oral phase of a child's development in that he felt that under- or over-gratification at that time would result in the person being 'stuck' in that emotional stage of development, unable to move on due to an abnormal dependence on others to maintain self-esteem. Much of Freud's work was discredited by Davison and Neal (1986), but many are still influenced by the psychoanalytical theories which focus on loss, over-dependence on outside approval and the internalization of anger.

Case study: Carole's story

Carole was a newly qualified staff nurse working in the day unit of a psychiatric unit. She felt that everything she did was undermined by Maureen, a senior staff nurse who had worked on the unit for some years. Maureen saw Carole as a threat and, although pleasant to her, constantly sought to keep her 'in her place'. When Carole mentioned this, she was told that she was over-reacting to the situation and it was also made clear to her by the ward manager that such comments were considered to be out of place when made by such a newly qualified member of staff. If she wanted to 'get on' she would have to keep her complaints to herself in the future.

Because Carole had a deep need for approval she did as she had been advised. Instead of improving the situation, this resulted in her internalizing her anger in order that people would like her and approve of the work she was doing. However, Maureen's attitude remained the same, and Carole continued to feel unfairly treated.

As time went on she began to experience feelings of anxiety and depression, both at work and at home. When they persisted she visited her GP, who did not prescribe antidepressants, but had a long talk with Carole who reluctantly admitted her problems at work. The doctor thought that she was suffering from the results of a personality clash and suggested that a new job might be the answer. Carole was reluctant to accept this because she felt that a problem with a manipulative colleague could not be the reason for her present condition. After all she was coping well with her work now . . . wasn't she? She would see if the depression would lift on its own before making any decision.

Shortly after this, a new ward manager took over the unit. She had known Carole during her training and recognized that she was not being allowed to fulfil her potential. She rearranged the unit so that each staff nurse became a team leader in her own right and over the next few weeks Carole began to feel better. As she was able to think more clearly and be more objective, she realized that it was not only the superficial problem that had made her feel ill but the fact that she had submerged her anger in order to cope with it. In time, her depression lifted completely and she was able to continue normal life.

Carole had experienced the effects of the internalizing of anger, but she had also suffered loss.

- What is the loss that Carole had undergone?
- Look back at your own experiences in life and try to identify instances of internalized anger. What was the result of this experience? If you have never experienced this, how did you handle anger? Have you any hints for others?

Cognitive theory

Beck (1976) believed that people become depressed because they feel responsible for every negative life event that has happened to them. He stated that people with depression learn a negative schema from which they view the world. When they encounter similar situations later, this negative schema is reactivated. They expect to fail, they magnify their failures, they minimize their successes (Atkinson, 1983). They feel that they can do nothing about their own helplessness and thus become victims of it.

Many studies in experimental psychology have shown that people's feelings can be influenced by how they perceive an event. The more control people have over the situation, the more their feelings of helplessness and hopelessness are reduced. Davison and Neal (1986) found that while negative or illogical thinking may cause individuals to believe that they have no control over the situation, this does not necessarily lead to depressive illness. Beck's theory has, however, encouraged therapists to work with and sort out these feelings when dealing with clients who are depressed.

Learned reinforcement theory

Seligman (1974) proposed a learned helplessness theory of depression. He suggested that when an individual responds to a stressful situation with an initial anxious response, this can lead to depression. Motivation to deal with a situation is undermined by a previous experience with lack of control, resulting in renewed inactivity in coping. When we are exposed to events which we cannot control, the experience affects our ability to learn about contingent relationships between future behaviour and outcomes. We have not learned by experience and this can produce emotional problems such as anxiety and depression.

There are certain factors which stand out as common in these three theories:

- Lack of control
- Feelings of helplessness
- Experience of loss
- Fear of failure

Everyone will experience some or all of these during the course of their lives. Some will respond to them with resultant depressive disorder and some will not. It would seem that no one theory can be used as an explanation. However, a great many people recovering from depressive episodes will identify with many of the points brought out in these theories. A very common factor appears to be *loss*. Loss can take many forms: for example, bereavement, divorce, or a loss of friendship, ambition, money, 'face', identity, confidence, past, future, looks, status and good physical health.

Biological theory

Although traditionally affective disorders were said to have no known biological cause, it is now thought that they *are* caused by complex biological and psychosocial factors. Research indicates that there is a strong familial connection, but it has not yet been proved that there is a direct genetic link. In the past it was suggested that the biological and metabolic processes of affective disorders needed to be investigated further before genetic research could progress. It has now been found that specific biological functions are altered in depression and that these alterations are present only when the mental state is abnormal. For example, it has been found that the Dexamethazone Suppression Test shows abnormal results when used on some patients and returns to normal when the patient recovers. It would seem that complex biological factors are involved in depression, for example catecholamine deficiency (particularly norepinephrine) has been implicated in depressive states and, in excess, in manic states. Several neurotransmitter systems may be involved, especially acetylcholine and serotonin. Studies have shown a very strong link between mental illness and hormones regulated by neurotransmitter systems.

Although generally accepted to be still 'in the stone age' in this area, scientists now accept that there is a strong biochemical link in depressive disorders. Family studies indicate a higher than expected incidence of depression and bipolar disorders. Twin studies have shown that when one identical twin has a mood disorder, the other twin is also affected in 67 per cent of cases. The rate reduces to 20 per cent in fraternal twins. Adoption studies have shown that a greater incidence of clinical depression is found among the biological parents of adopted adults with bipolar disorder than in their adoptive parents.

Let us now attempt to pull together the strands of the explanations just given, using another case history.

Case study: Jane's story

Jane was the only child of the unhappy marriage of Sam and Margaret, which ended when Jane was seven years old. From that time she was cared for by her father and his parents who doted on her while at the same time trying not to spoil her. By the time Jane was ten both her grandparents had died and her world was turned upside down when Sam married Elsa, a woman ten years his junior. Elsa had suffered a very poor relationship with her own father, who had been very strict, and she saw the closeness of Jane and Sam as 'rather odd'. She was also jealous of her step-daughter, on whom she imposed strict rules and regulations which Jane had difficulty in keeping. Elsa scolded and slapped; Jane pleaded with her father to intervene; Sam 'sat on the fence'. He loved his daughter and he did not want to lose a second wife, so he refused to take sides when everybody was together, but took the side of whoever of the two was with him when alone. He did, on occasion, try to get fairer treatment for Jane, but gave in when Elsa insisted that she should have 'the last word' on discipline. At such times, he consoled Jane with bars of chocolate hidden under her pillow and illicit trips downstairs to watch television later than usual when Elsa was out for the evening.

As would be expected, this approach pushed Jane and Elsa further apart rather than closer together. When she was fourteen it was agreed that Jane could go and live with her mother, if her father could find out where she lived. Sam had been awarded sole custody of Jane after the divorce and Margaret had agreed to forego her visiting rights when it was explained to her that Jane became very distressed after seeing her mother and would prefer not to see her at all in the future. (It may be said that Jane was not consulted on the matter and was simply told that it was her mother who had decided not to see her any more.) True to form, Sam told Elsa and Jane that he could find no trace of Margaret, a fact that he later admitted to be totally untrue. At the age of seventeen Jane left home to become a nurse, Sam relented and contacted his ex-wife. He told her that their daughter would like to hear from her.

In later life Jane found that, although she still loved her father, she resented his behaviour much more than that of her step-mother, whom she got on with quite well once they no longer lived under the same roof. She saw her father as a weak man who had always put his own needs before hers. Jane's mother told her that she had always been in contact with Sam and that he had given her to understand that Jane and Elsa 'got on like a house on fire'. No mentioned had ever been made of Jane wanting to go live with Margaret, or the fact that there was so much discord within the home.

Jane moved in with her mother and step-father, enjoyed the company of her young half-brothers and got on with her life. She did not hold any undue resentment and was just glad that a very unhappy period of her life was over. She began training as a nurse and went on to have a very successful career. She married when she was twenty-five, had a son when she was twenty-eight and, at the age of thirty-five, although suffering two miscarriages in the intervening period, completed her family when she gave birth to a daughter. She continued to work as a senior nurse, combining a career and motherhood; her husband, Paul, supported her in this decision. They also agreed that their children would be brought up on a healthy mixture of love and discipline. Jane was determined that her children should not have the same unhappy experiences that she had had and Paul's only caution was that they should not over-indulge the children in order to achieve this.

Sarah, the youngest child was what most people would call 'a bit of a madam', but gave a lot, as well as taking it, and was fairly popular at school. She loved her mother dearly and confrontations were soon forgotten, although those with her father tended to be taken a bit more seriously. Generally, she was a normal child . . . whatever that is.

Jake, who was seven years older than Sarah, caused both his parents heartbreak 'from the word go'. He was a colicky baby who went on to become a demanding and aggressive toddler. By the time he started school he had been expelled from play group and done little to redeem himself, although Paul and Jane always tried to support him as best they could. By the time Jake was fourteen, Jane had lost count of the times she had been telephoned at work because the teachers could not cope with Jake's aggressive, bullying behaviour, especially towards women staff members. Psychologists could not help because they could not find any 'family dysfunction', apart from that caused by Jake himself.

His behaviour at home was no better, and Paul and Jane found that only very strict discipline kept him under any control at all. This was what Jane had undergone herself, and had been determined to avoid. Paul had been brought up with love and kindness and felt alien to the whole situation. Jane demanded that Paul punish Jake, but Paul felt only able to do this within reasonable boundaries. He refused to 'nag'. Jane thought that her husband should do more to protect her from the verbal onslaughts of their son, although on the rare occasion that Jake raised his hand to her, Paul made it very clear that this behaviour was not acceptable within their family. It was after one such occasion that social services were invited into the family because it was felt that Jake could not live at home any longer.

The social worker tried to get Jake to return to school (he was now in his last year and refused to go in at all), and also decided not to put Jake into sheltered accommodation because he felt that the boy was under no risk. He also told Jake that his behaviour was totally unacceptable, and that if he did not want to 'toe the line' he should take himself off and give his family a break! The boy was shocked by this total support for his parents and gradually his behaviour started to improve. He is eighteen now and he has held down a job since he officially left school at sixteen. He gives his parents board money, stays out late when he feels like it and generally treats the world at large, including his family, with a fair degree of respect. Sometimes he is obnoxious, of course but, as Jane says, 'What teenager isn't?'

So what is the point of this story? When Jake was fourteen Jane began to exhibit signs of depression; she became irritable, tearful and lost motivation. You may think that this was not surprising under the circumstances, but it should be remembered that Jake was only a part of Jane's life, and the rest of it was fairly gratifying. She loved her husband and drew much comfort from her daughter. She was highly successful in her job, which she enjoyed immensely, and she and Paul had a good support network among friends and family. She knew that her depression was caused by Jake but at first refused antidepressant therapy, stating that she could see no point in treating the disorder with chemicals when the only cure would be for Jake to grow up and leave home. Eventually she became so ill that she had to take several weeks off work, and at this point she accepted the fluoxetine therapy which brought her to the level where she could function normally. She found that she became more tolerant of Jake and stopped bouncing his aggression back to him. She decided that it was Jake who had the problem and that he would have to take the consequences. He could play silly games but she and Paul did not have to drag themselves down and join in with him. She also became more tolerant of Paul's difficulties in handling Jake and felt much more able to work with her husband, while appreciating that he, like her, had his limitations.

Because one of Jane's main worries had been the effect that her brother's behaviour would have on Sarah, she refused to have confrontations in front of her. Instead, she would make an excuse and take the child out of the house and leave Jake to get over his temper tantrum on his own. When social services stepped in and gave Paul and Jane the emotional support that they needed, Jane was already quite able to take on board the idea that Jake should live peaceably at home or leave. As we have seen, Jake's behaviour improved a great deal after this and now the family live in comparative harmony. It would seem that Jake's teenage hormones settled down, his mother's depression lifted, and they were able to deal with their relationship far more appropriately. Nowadays Jane's biggest worry about her son is the universal one . . . the health hazard of Jake's room!

When looking at Jane's story carefully, it becomes apparent that many parts of it fit areas of the different theories on depression. Let us look at this more closely.

Jane's story: psychoanalytical theory

To recap, the important points of this theory are loss, over-dependence on outside approval and the internalizing of anger. In Jane's case we know she suffered loss on several counts. She had lost her self-respect because she had to ask for professional intervention to enable her and Paul to deal with Jake. Importantly, she had lost the son she had wished for, along with the harmonious parent–child relationship which was so important to her.

- What other losses has Jane undergone?

I do not feel that Jane exhibited signs of over-dependence on outside approval to any great degree, although it was very important to her that the social worker realized that she was not to blame for Jake's behaviour and that her household functioned fairly normally.

- Is it okay to have a moderate dependency on outside approval? Cite some of the examples from your own life.

Most mothers learn to express their anger appropriately when dealing with their children. Jane exhibited a degree of internalizing of anger because the source of her anger (Jake's behaviour) was so long-standing that to have acknowledged it constantly would not have been acceptable to her.

Jane's story: cognitive theory

The key phrases of cognitive theory in relation to this case study are: 'magnifying failure', 'minimizing success' and 'adopting a negative schema' when confronted with a situation similar to the one when these factors were first experienced.

- Compare these elements to those in Jane's story.

Jane's story: learned reinforcement theory

Jane's story demonstrates this theory well. When she was a child she responded to the parenting she received from her father and Elsa with a high degree of anxiety. She felt helpless because it was beyond her power to change things; indeed, when she tried to, first by asking her father for his support and then by asking to go to live with her mother, she was thwarted. She also felt anxious and hopeless because of the high degree of bullying involved in her relationship with Elsa. When Jake displayed a pronounced tendency to bully her, albeit verbally, she once again experienced the original feelings surrounding her childhood situation. Paul's inability to protect her was also a compounding factor. It was when Jake's bullying started that Jane first began to display symptoms of anxiety and depression.

Jane's story: biological theory

Jane originally thought that only by 'getting rid' of the problem would she cure her depressive condition. She was surprised that, as a result of taking the antidepressant therapy, she felt far more objective and able to cope with a *continuing situation*. In other words, the situation had not changed that much but her tolerance level within it had changed. This continued even when she had stopped the medication. It would seem indicative, if not proven, that Jane's biochemical make-up had been altered by the continuing stress that she had undergone; once this had been corrected, she was more able to cope.

Jane's story indicates how depression, in many cases, is multi-causal. Just because one theory does not fit completely does not mean that theory is wrong; it simply means that theories are like people – complicated!

- List the areas of loss which may be particularly relevant to the situation of a new mother. Explain how the fear of failure can affect her, taking into account the pressures placed upon her by modern society. How do these pressures differ from those of 40 years ago?

REFERENCES

American Psychiatric Association (1987) *Statistical Diagnosis of Mental Disorders* (3rd revised edn). Washington: APA.

Atkinson, R.L. (1983) *Introduction to Psychology* (8th edn). London: Harcourt Brace Jovanovich.

Beck, A. (1976) *Cognitive Therapy and the Emotional Disorders.* New York: International Universities Press.

Brown, G.W. and Harris, T. (1978) *Social Origins of Depression.* London: Tavistock.

Davison, G. and Neal, J. (1986) *Abnormal Psychology* (4th edn). Chichester: Wiley.

Freud, S. (1917) *Mourning and Melancholia.* Collected Papers (Vol. 4). London: Hogarth Press.

Hirshfeld, R.M.A. (1994) 'Major depression, dysthymia and depressive personality disorder', *British Journal of Psychiatry*, 165 (supplement 26–30).

Seligman, L.E.P. (1974) 'Depression and learned helplessness', in R.J. Freidman and M.M. Katz (eds), *The Psychology of Depression: Contemporary Theory and Research.* Washington: Winston.

World Health Organisation (1992) *The ICD–10 Classifications of Mental and Behavioural Disorders.* Geneva: WHO.

3

ASSOCIATED DISORDERS

EATING DISORDERS

While there is no evidence to suggest that eating disorders are more likely to occur after the birth of a baby, I feel that it is important for health professionals to be aware of some of the psychological factors of eating disorders which may be seen as similar to those surrounding general depressive disturbances. They will be quicker to recognize and differentiate symptoms of eating disorders, should they arise from postnatal depression. Several of the precipitating factors that influence the onset of *bulimia*, such as stress, will be present during the early months following childbirth, so it is possible, but not proven, that this may be a critical time for vulnerable individuals.

The eating disorder I consider most relevant to depressive illness is that of *bulimia.* However, as it is so closely akin to its sister-condition of *anorexia nervosa*, it is important that both of these conditions are understood. Problems like depression, anxiety and personality disorder can all present simultaneously with *anorexia nervosa.* Since depression can also cause weight loss, and this may be confused with *anorexia nervosa*, especially in younger women, when a woman loses her appetite she may be described as anorexic and, hearing this term, she may assume that the health professionals consider her to have a mental problem connected with dieting and food refusal. It is important that she realizes that *anorexia* simply means loss of appetite, as opposed to *anorexia nervosa* which is a well-defined serious illness, which may not involve loss of appetite even though the sufferer severely restricts her food intake. Depression and alcohol misuse often coincide with *bulimia* and a borderline personality disorder seems sometimes to be a factor.

Anorexia nervosa

Anorexia nervosa usually begins in adolescence and young adulthood, however it can occur at any age. The shedding of body weight and restriction of food intake gives the woman a feeling of control. It is more common in young women than young men and is usually associated with *distorted body image*. What often starts as the shedding of a few pounds, progresses to self-starvation as the person continues to see an already slim/underweight body as fat and unattractive. False perception of body image may actually increase as the sufferer becomes more emaciated. The effect of starvation upon the brain is thought to cause difficulties in estimating size, even of inanimate objects and distances between them. Sufferers do still have very good appetites and will tell you that they feel really well but just do not feel like eating much, or are on a diet. If forced to sit down to a meal, they will go to some lengths to hide food or cause an argument so that they have a legitimate reason to leave the table. Because they know that their weight-reducing behaviour is abnormal, and does not meet with approval, they will do other things secretly. These may commonly include taking laxatives to cause intestinal hurry, thus preventing adequate absorption of food. They may also induce vomiting directly after a meal and take diuretics to further reduce body weight by ridding the body of water. Many also indulge in physical exercise to an obsessive degree.

Causes: cognitive behavioural model

The concept behind the cognitive behavioural theory is that the individual 'over-values' ideas about shape and weight. Any excessive dieting and exercising the individual does is secondary to this. The cognitive behavioural therapist sees the values and beliefs of the individual's self-imposed rules, which are implicit, influencing the ways in which she evaluates her experience of herself and her world, and attributes meaning to it. Furthermore, the sufferer exhibits certain dysfunctional thinking, which is reflected in the absolute nature of her belief in regard to her shape and size. An example of this would be the belief that eating an extra slice of bread indicates the individual's total lack of self-control.

Causes: socio-cultural model

This is a very popular explanation of *anorexia nervosa.* It suggests that society considers slimness to be the most important feature of female beauty. Anorexia is seen to be encouraged by the relentless images of thin models, constantly being sold to us by the media. Slimming products are pushed at us and we are encouraged to equate thinness and youth with glamour, fame and success. When women compare themselves to such images they all too frequently feel that they are failing. The pressure directed at women to be thin may precipitate the development of anorexia. Any treatment must take into account the way in which an individual's psychology absorbs and interprets cultural values. This is important as the approach to treatment does not allow blame on strictly individual problems without taking into account the social and cultural influences on the deviant behaviour displayed by the sufferers.

However, the socio-cultural model cannot account for the fact that many individuals do not develop anorexia, although they are exposed to the same environment. Neither does it take into account the fact that anorexia is not a new disease. Brumberg has documented the historical roots of anorexia (Brumberg, 1988). In Europe between 1200 and 1500 a significant number of women refused food in order to express their 'female holiness'. Bell draws some striking parallels between these 'holy anorexics' and the anorexics of today (Bell, 1985). He notes that the self-starvation typically started in adolescence in order to resolve feelings of unworthiness and doubt. Nowadays we may think of this as *lack of self-esteem.*

Causes: psychodynamic model

The most influential work within this model is probably that of Hille Bruch. She maintains that the basic deficit in anorexia has its roots in the lack of recognition of cues initiated by the child in the very early mother–child relationship. The result is an over-compliant, passive child who has little sense of self, identity and autonomy, and who finds the sexual impulses of adolescence a dangerous challenge. She then relieves her anxiety over *losing control* by the repression of sexual desire and starvation. (Anorexia also causes the cessation of periods – that is, denial of sexuality.)

Causes: systemic model

Within this model problems are understood as arising in the context of particular interactions between people. According to Minuchin *et al.* (1978), four factors are typical of the anorectic family: *enmeshment*, *over-protectiveness*, *rigidity* and *avoidance*. Minuchin explored the types of environment which encourage passive methods of defiance. He describes the anorectic family as controlling, perfectionist and non-confrontational – adjectives which he also applies to the psychosomatic family. He considers the individual's behaviour to be both caused and causative, and emphasizes the interpersonal aspects of anorexia, that is, a phenomenon of regulation between an over-protective parent and a developing adolescent struggling to assert her autonomy.

Links with depression?

There is no proven direct connection between depressive illness and *anorexia nervosa* but some research suggests that self-starvation may be a way of exercising power and control when young people feel helpless or out of control. This would rarely be a conscious reason for 'dieting' but can happen when a diet is embarked upon by an individual who then finds herself completely in control of this particular area of her existence. If other areas of her life are being managed by outside events or other people, this 'power' can then become addictive and difficult to relinquish. This may well increase feelings of euphoria as the 'pounds drop off'.

Anorexia nervosa often starts soon after a stressful life event, but it has to be noted that nearly all teenagers will have to face several new experiences, many of which may be stressful. Some that may, by coincidence, precede the onset of the disorder include leaving school, starting work or college, leaving home and making and breaking relationships. Many of these events can be quite frightening, especially when combined with the physical changes taking place as an ever-present reminder of approaching adulthood. Losing weight and reversing physical changes (in advanced cases menstruation ceases) may make returning to pre-puberty seem a safe alternative to adulthood for some girls.

- Consider the issue of lack of self-esteem. How is this also involved in the aetiology of depressive disturbance?

Bulimia nervosa

Bulimia is an eating disorder related to anorexia nervosa. The biggest difference between the two disorders is that people with bulimia have impulsive binges of massive over-eating followed by self-induced vomiting and/or excessive purging, using laxatives. This disorder does not usually lead to massive weight loss, in fact the weight is often normal. Bulimic people have a fear of fatness, as opposed to the anorexic nervosa's fear of normal weight. The condition rarely causes fatality, as opposed to the three out of one hundred of anorexia nervosas who die.

A study in Switzerland found that only 4 per cent of people in their late twenties, who were picked randomly from the population, were binge-eaters, two-thirds of them women (Vollrath, 1992). One in five of the group were worried about their weight and one in ten were on diets, although only a few of them were overweight. Of the dieters, most were women. Of the overweight people, most were men.

Symptoms

Binge-eating is the main feature of this disorder. Typical binges are usually carried out in secret and the complete contents of a fridge may be emptied in the process. It has been known for 40,000 calories to be consumed in just one day. The content of the feast can be anything edible, including whole loaves of bread, family-size meat pies, cream cakes, etc. Between binges most sufferers diet strictly, or at least are careful what they eat. Menstrual cycle is usually normal.

Soon after eating, sufferers usually make themselves sick by putting their fingers down their throat. The entire contents of the stomach will be disgorged in this way, bringing some of the stomach acid with it. If done often enough, this can be detrimental to dental health. Dehydration and mineral imbalances can be dangerous if vomiting persists, and loss of potassium may cause serious cardiac problems.

Psychological problems

Sufferers have a fear of being fat and may sometimes be slightly overweight. They do not have the distorted perception of body image common to the anorexia nervosa sufferer. It has been said by some bulimics that they binge to hold back unpleasant emotions. Many non-sufferers should be able to identify with this when we think of the 'reaching for the bar of chocolate' syndrome, which is common to many people when they are feeling a bit 'low'. Because the 'binge' produces intense feelings of self-disgust and physical discomfort, the desire to vomit follows, which in turn is followed by feelings of relief and elation.

Causes

Very little research has been done on the causes of bulimia nervosa. It would seem that most bulimics have been trying to lose weight before the symptoms start. Depression and alcohol misuse often coincide with bulimia and a borderline personality disorder seems to be a factor in some sufferers. Another factor that researchers keep finding among people with bulimia is a history of sexual abuse. Up to half the women with eating disorders say that they have been sexually abused, or subjected to unwanted sexual experiences in the past; most of these women are suffering from bulimia, rather than anorexia nervosa.

Sufferers usually say that a bout of binging will be precipitated by an unpleasant emotion such as depression, anxiety or frustration. When the person begins to binge the emotion is eclipsed, and then the secondary emotion of shame, self-disgust, etc. is dispelled by the action of vomiting. The end result is a feeling of elation. It is very difficult to resist the urge to repeat the pattern and each episode involves a cycle which cannot be broken.

Finally, acute stress can be a trigger for bulimia nervosa, whether this is found in the home, at work or as a result of social pressures (Groves and Pennell, 1995).

Treatment of bulimia nervosa

Before any psychological treatment can commence, it is important that any mineral and electrolyte imbalances are treated, and this may well involve treatment in hospital. A women who has undergone past sexual abuse may need psychotherapy, but others usually respond well to behaviour therapy. One or more of the following may be employed:

- Stress management training: to find more appropriate ways of dealing with stress.

- Behaviour modification: to explain and encourage healthier eating patterns.
- Cognitive therapy: to look at the way the mind perceives problems and to retrain it in the way it approaches them. This therapy is particularly useful when the sufferer is also depressed.

Although behaviour therapy is very effective in the long term, it may be useful to use antidepressants in the short term. Fluoxetine (Prozac) is a member of the SSRI group (selective serotonin reuptake inhibitors) and is useful in treating this disorder. It works by increasing the concentration in the brain of the chemical serotonin which is thought to be important in controlling mood and regulating eating.

THE STRESS CONNECTION

Stress can be seen as the influences either from within an individual or arising from pressures in the environment, which interfere or prevent basic needs being met, or disrupt or threaten to disrupt an individual's homeostatic balance. Thus we can see that stress appears in many guises, such as self-criticism, illness or too many demands on oneself and one's resources (Smith, 1987). there are three principal categories of stress:

1. Loss, or threat of loss. This can be in any area of our lives, including loss of 'face', employment, ambition, loved ones, etc.
2. Actual or threatened injury to our bodies.
3. Frustration of our basic biological drives – the need for shelter, warmth, food, social networks and support, sexual relationships.

Rapoport (1965) made the distinction between stress and a life-crisis situation. A crisis is seen to have the potential to allow us to 'grow' because it causes an individual to adapt and search for new behaviours. It may, in fact, raise the individual's level of mental health. Stress, on the other hand, tends to reduce one's level of mental health. This is because it is a subjective experience from which one either emerges to survive, or succumbs to the ensuing pressure.

We know that stress has different effects on different people and that it can often be detrimental to general well-being. If we consider the Holmes Rahe Life Stress Inventory as a tool to connect levels of stress to the likelihood of future health breakdown, we will see that if stress is not handled appropriately it can lead to quite serious problems.

Holmes Rahe Life Stress Inventory

As we look at the life stress inventory we will be able to identify many points which mothers will be able to identify with. Many would have a high score even if they had no obvious problems. Let us pick possible events out. Remember that we are looking at events which have happened within one year, so we will start from a point of a family with a baby aged six weeks.

SCORE (out of 100)	LIFE EVENT
7	Marriage (let us include 'setting up home' with partner)
12	Pregnancy
14	Gaining a new member of the family
16	Major changes in financial state
18	Changing to a different line of work
22	Major changes in responsibility at work
25	Outstanding personal achievement
26	Wife ceasing work outside the home
31	Major changes in working hours and conditions
34	Major change in type and/or amount of recreation
36	Major change in social activities
37	Taking on a small mortgage or a loan
38	Major changes in sleeping habits

The total for this estimate, based on a probable first-time mother, is a massive 359. An unsafe level is considered to be that over 100. This score implies an 80 per cent chance of a major health breakdown within the next two years. As though this was not enough, add a few other possible events such as sexual difficulties or mortgage foreclosure and many problems are evident. It is a wonder that all women do not become ill after the birth of their baby.

- Why do you think this is? What other factors may be relevant? Discuss.

Stressors

Many stressors can be identified and I have selected two of the more obvious ones – quantitative overload and qualitative overload – to discuss in this section.

Quantitative overload (also described as *time urgency*). The individual has too much work to do within a set time. For example, I am writing a book and it has to be finished by November. I have 70,000 words to write and I have completed 20,000. It is now July. Result? I have quantitative overload.

Qualitative Overload. The work required exceeds the abilities of the individual. This may be due to technical or intellectual limitations.

Sometimes quantitative and qualitative overload combine and this is well demonstrated in the area of decision-making. To make a decision correctly, several factors have to be allowed for. These include the relative importance of the decision, having the correct information, and having sufficient time. If any of these factors is missing the individual may experience a rise in stress levels. If this only happens infrequently, it is not likely that much harm will be done, but if it is a common occurrence, stress related symptoms may result.

Occupation and stress

This often centres on the inhibition or thwarting of attainment. It may be described as 'work underload' and leads to occupational frustration. It can be caused by several factors or a combination of factors. Some examples are:

- Job ambiguity. For example, unclear work goals, confusion surrounding responsibility, unclear working procedures and lack of feedback. The latter, in particular, can cause high levels of anxiety (anxiety states).
- Role conflict. The job may conflict with family role, religious beliefs, societal values, etc.
- Lack of career development guidance. For example, when an individual is not given the opportunity to use or learn new skills, or to maximize career opportunities by utilizing appropriate guidance and training opportunities.
- Occupational change. For example, promotion, redundancy,

changes in the work place with the introduction of new technology, etc. Even when a change is welcome it causes a degree of stress, so it is important to avoid too many changes all at the same time. Unfortunately, changes in work patterns can sometimes coincide with changes of home, friends and immediate environment. This situation applies well to a new mother who has just moved house, given up her job, lost her old friends and has qualitative and quantitative overload!

- Physical environment. This can include anything in the environment which the individual finds stressful and has difficulty coping with. For most of us noise levels will be important. We will also want a degree of comfort which will include an appropriate temperature, adequate lighting, housing and sanitation provision.

Effects of stress

These are widespread, and can be split into three areas: cognitive, behavioural and physiological.

Cognitive: Distorted thinking, lowering of intellectual functioning, poor verbal communication, unproductive (although 'busy'), anxiety-generating patterns of thinking, inability to make decisions.
Behavioural: Decreased performance level, passivity, avoidance of stressful situations.
Physiological: Increased heart rate, raised blood pressure, increased muscular tension, slowing of digestive system.

Signs and symptoms of stress

These match the same group as the effects of stress.

Cognitive: Decreased intellectual functioning, decreased self confidence, indecisiveness, decreased libido, poor coping ability, nightmares, anger, irritability.
Behavioural: Withdrawal, isolation, sleep disturbance, eating disturbance, crying, poor work performance, unproductiveness, poor time keeping/absenteeism, aggression, nervous habits, obsessional behaviour, verbal dysfunction, drinking and drug use may be used to avoid or escape from certain situations.
Physiological symptoms. These can be divided into the muscular, cardiovascular and gastrointestinal systems.

- *Muscular system*: tension/cramps, tension headache, chest pain, tremor, spasmodic dysmenorrhoea.
- *Cardiovascular system*: migraine, palpitations, tachycardia, increased blood pressure, pelvic pain, peripheral coldness and numbness, tinnitus, flushing/pallor, congestive dysmenorrhoea.
- *Gastrointestinal system*: nausea, 'butterflies', ulcers/indigestion, irritable bowel syndrome, appetite problems.

- Other symptoms include: runny nose, insomnia, sexual dysfunction, breathlessness/hyperventilation, sweating, skin disorders, hair loss, blurred vision, menstrual and reproductive problems, immune system impairment.

Cognitive distortions

These are often a feature in *stress related disorders* and some of them will be familiar to many or all of us. Many people tend to suffer from one or more of this type of distortion at some time in their lives to a slight degree, but when it/they become a major part of the personality, it/they cannot be considered to be desirable cognitive functioning.

1. **'All-or-nothing' thinking**. Anxious people see things in black and white categories. If their performance falls short of perfection, they see themselves as a total failure.
2. **Over-generalization**. Anxious people see a single negative event as a never-ending pattern.
3. **Mental filter**. Anxious people pick out a single negative detail and dwell on it exclusively, so that their vision of reality becomes darkened, like the drop of ink that colours the whole beaker of water.
4. **Disqualifying the positive**. Anxious people reject experiences by insisting that 'they don't count' for some reason or other. In this way they can maintain a negative belief that is contradicted by everyday experiences.
5. **Jumping to conclusions**. Anxious people make a negative interpretation even though there are no definite facts that convincingly support the conclusion.
   (a) Mind reading: Arbitrarily conclude that someone is reacting negatively to them, and do not bother to check this out.

(b) Fortune-teller error: Anticipate that things will turn out badly, and feel convinced that the prediction is already an established fact.

6. **Magnification or minimization**. Anxious people exaggerate the importance of events (such as their mistake or someone else's achievement), or they inappropriately shrink things until they appear tiny (their own desirable qualities or the other person's imperfections).
7. **Emotional reasoning**. Anxious people assume that their negative emotions necessarily reflect the way things really are – 'I feel, therefore it must be true'.
8. **'Should' statements**. Anxious people try to motivate themselves with 'shoulds' and 'shouldn'ts' as if they had to be whipped and punished before they could be expected to do anything. 'Musts' and 'oughts' are also offenders. The emotional consequence is guilt. When they direct 'should' statements towards others, they feel anger, frustration and resentment.
9. **Labelling and mislabelling**. This is an extreme form of over-generalization. Instead of describing their error, they attach a negative label to themselves – 'I'm a loser'. When someone else's behaviour rubs them the wrong way, they attach a negative label to her – 'She's a pain'. Mislabelling involves describing an event with language that is highly coloured and emotionally loaded.
10. **Personalization**. Anxious people see themselves as the cause of some negative event for which, in fact, they were not primarily responsible.

■ Look back over the last ten points and try to identify with at least one point. When you have done this, consider whether this trait is exaggerated when you are going through a period of anxiety. Try to pinpoint an occasion when this has happened.

NON-ASSERTION AS A CAUSE OF STRESS

It is undoubtedly true that individuals who have a problem with asserting themselves are very likely to find themselves in anxiety-producing scenarios and often will be unable to do anything to help themselves to alter the situation. Non-assertive people have problems recognizing their own rights as individuals, and will often 'bottle up' their feelings rather than create a scene. They will usually agree with other people, in deference to their own opinion, especially if the other party is in a more powerful position. They do not feel at ease stating honest disagreements and they are extremely sensitive to disapproval. Saying 'no' or 'why?' is almost impossible for them and this can lead to a likelihood of being pushed around by others. They can rarely accept a compliment without embarrassment and may find eye contact difficult. They are unable to talk positively about themselves in a positive manner and have difficulty in asking for what they want and insisting on fair treatment. Some people, while not 'non-assertive' as described above, have problems with assertiveness that results in aggressive behaviour. As this reaction rarely gets an individual what she wants, or where she wants to be, this 'mal-assertive' approach causes stress/anxiety problems of its own.

■ Why would aggressive people become anxious and stressed?

As already stated, lack of assertiveness will undoubtedly lead to stress in most people. If we look at the indices of non-assertion, it will become apparent why.

Indices of non-assertion

1. Inability to express all manner of emotions, both pleasant and unpleasant, in an open, honest and direct manner.
2. Inability to recognize one's own personal rights.
3. Inability to state honest opinions with ease.
4. Inability to insist on fair treatment.
5. Inability to ask 'why?' or say 'no'.
6. Inability to ask for what one wants.
7. Extreme sensitivity to disapproval.
8. Excessive agreement with the wishes of more powerful individuals.
9. Inability to give or accept compliments without embarrassment.
10. Inability to express an opinion.
11. Likelihood of being pushed around by others.
12. Inability to express anger.
13. Inability to talk about oneself in a positive manner.
14. Low frequency eye contact.

15. A weak voice or poor word fluency which causes others not to pay due regard to what one says.
16. Bottling up feelings instead of creating a scene.

- Match the indices listed on the left to the events listed on the right. What effects will the lack of assertiveness have on the individual involved in each scenario? (Role play may be useful here.)

Indices	**Situation**
2, 4, 11, 12	Cary is a new mother who is concerned because her six-week-old baby has diarrhoea. When she phones the surgery, at 9 a.m., the receptionist will only offer to 'fit her in' after afternoon surgery. Cary is unhappy with this and tells the receptionist that she would like to see the doctor after morning surgery. She is told that this is not possible as he has urgent home visits to do. Cary asks if the baby can have a home visit. The receptionist asks her if she would really like to prevent the doctor from getting any lunch. Her manner is patronizing. Cary agrees to attend following afternoon surgery.
1, 3, 7, 12, 13	On arriving at the surgery that evening, Cary is subjected to intense verbal disapproval from the GP, who tells her that she should have brought the baby to see him earlier on in the day. He lectures her on the dangers of dehydration. Cary tries to explain, but gives up when it seems that he is not listening to her at all. She leaves the surgery feeling very angry. The next day the health visitor arrives to see if the baby is improving. The GP had voiced concern over the child, but also about Cary, whom he realized was very upset and angry. He asked the health visitor to check that everything was all right. The health visitor asks what happened. Cary feels herself going very red and her head starts to pound. She will not tell the health visitor what has happened, but does state that she is

very unhappy with the service that she has received from her GP and will be looking for a new one in the near future. She asks the health visitor whom she would recommend, but will not discuss the previous day's events except to state that she feels quite ill. She begins to cry. She knows that this is the only thing that will make her feel better, as it has done in the past when people have upset her. She wishes that she could confide in the health visitor but she finds expressing her feelings very difficult and, in any case, she feels so silly when she cries.

There are many women like Cary, who suffer the results of non-assertive behaviour. Before we can begin to help these women we need to be clear about the assertive behaviours that they should be encouraged to acquire (see p. 136).

PANIC ATTACKS

I choose this forum to discuss 'panic' attacks because around 9,000,000 people in the UK suffer from them every day and it does seem to be indicated that, as well as a connection with stress, there is a connection with depressive disorder on two counts:

1. Antidepressant medications seem to have a very successful effect in combating the 'panic attack' syndrome.
2. It is important that professionals, and the general public, become aware that the widespread use of beta-blockers to combat the disabling symptoms of this condition can, in itself, be a cause of depression because of their widespread mode of action. GPs should be dissuaded from the beta-blocker as a cure for panic attacks. Experts are currently warning that they are not effective on a long-term basis.

People suffering from panic attacks usually have a history of stress, phobias (such as acrophobia) and sudden lifestyle changes. The physical symptoms include pins and needles in the hands and feet, dizziness and fainting, a sensation of choking, a tight feeling in the stomach, trembling, tachycardia and palpitations, and/or chest pains. People commonly believe that they are going to have a heart attack and this probably partly explains why a very high percentage of people taken to coronary care units are found not to have any coronary disorder.

Some counsellors attached to GP surgeries do have the expertise to deal with patients suffering these attacks, but when this is not the situation it may, in many cases, be appropriate for them to be referred to a psychologist. There is still a huge role to be played by members of the PHCT. These patients need continuing reassurance, and their relatives often need a great deal of support also. The attacks can be disabling enough to render people incapable of working; they can incur long-term sick leave and sometimes actual loss of employment. When this happens financial advice may also need to be on hand. A vague wave in the direction of the social security department is not generally reassuring enough for someone as ill as these patients. It may be appropriate for the relatives to be counselled and the disorder explained to them in quite a lot of detail. It cannot be easy to live with a loved one who is always 'about to have a heart attack' when an individual does not understand the reason for these symptoms. Some technical understanding can do a lot to help relatives and friends to deal with the attacks when they are on the spot. Also remember that it is up to you to make the explanations understandable to people, no matter what their educational or cultural background may be. Diagrams may be of use to explain cause and effect.

Case study: Sue's story

Sue Smith is 40 years old and is married to Mark. They have two children. Sue works as a graphic artist. Sue suffered a 'panic attack' on her way home from work in March 1992. For several months Mark had been suggesting that she might be depressed and, with her consent, had made an appointment for her to see her GP a couple of weeks before the initial incident took place. However, Sue had been extremely busy at work and had cancelled the appointment. At this time she had begun to feel that she was simply 'out of condition' and made the decision to give up smoking and to 'take better care of herself' generally. To enable her to do this, Sue made another appointment with the doctor and was started on a course of nicotine patches.

For the first week she did very well, although she would have admitted to vague feelings of stress. The nicotine patches were very effective and she was able to avoid the extreme withdrawal symptoms that she had suffered during previous attempts to quit smoking. On the day in question she had had a rather stressful and busy day during an unusually demanding week at work. The attack came on very suddenly and began with an adrenaline surge which started in Sue's feet and rushed up to engulf the whole of her body. She then became aware of a pounding in her chest and difficulty in breathing. She noticed a numbness in her hands and mouth, and during the next 12 hours she passed copious amounts of urine. From the beginning of the attack she was extremely afraid and thought that she was seriously ill. She arrived home and was driven to the accident and emergency department by a very worried Mike.

There, nothing could be found untoward apart from a tachycardia of 140 per minute, which the staff explained was probably caused by general fear, and Sue was discharged. The following morning Mike called out one of the GPs from the group practice, a locum called Dr Gregory, who, after examining Sue thoroughly, said that she had probably suffered a panic attack. He prescribed beta-blockers and suggested bed rest for at least two days followed by a fortnight's sick leave. It was decided that the nicotine patches were possibly the culprit. The patches were stopped and Sue reached for her cigarette packet. Dr Gregory said that she should try to stop smoking again, but not until a later date. Both Sue and Mike felt relieved that an explanation had been given and resolved to relax a little now that they knew that Sue's life was not in danger and that she would be returning to work the following week.

Two days later Sue was admitted into Coronary Care with chest pains, breathing difficulties and the tachycardia which had continued almost unabated despite the beta-blockers. After two days she was given the 'all clear', and discharged home, only to be admitted again a few days later. Once again she was discharged and the beta-blockers were increased. The following Monday she went back to work, only to be sent home when her symptoms returned. By this time her usual GP, Dr Harvey, was convinced that there was a severe physical problem and referred Sue urgently to the consultant specializing in cardiology. Over the next few weeks several more tests were carried out, but the end result was that Sue had a perfectly normal heart and was generally found to be in extremely good health. When asked how she felt at that time, she said that it would have been a relief to be told that she had some physical illness to explain her very frightening symptoms.

She was still looking for explanations when she visited the GP again three months after the original attack. The family had been abroad on holiday and it had been a total disaster due to the fact that, after a short reprieve, Sue's symptoms had returned in spasmodic but frequent episodes. To make matters worse, in between times she had no energy, no motivation and was later to admit that the idea of suicide had 'vaguely crossed my mind'. She was still taking the beta-blockers and felt that any depression was due to the fact that she felt so ill and exhausted. Mike accompanied his wife into the doctor's surgery, determined that she be made to face up to her growing depressive illness. By this time he felt that he was also in danger of becoming ill, simply due to worry, if help was not forthcoming. He felt aware that he was developing a harder attitude to avoid this happening, and that he was growing impatient with Sue's refusal to believe that the cause of her physical problems was psychological.

Mike need not have worried; Dr Gregory was once again standing in for Dr Harvey and he did not mince his words. Even the 'getting tougher by the minute' Mike flinched when the doctor looked straight at Sue and told her that she was suffering from anxiety neurosis and explained that this often presented itself in the form of panic attacks. After being counselled at some length, Sue accepted that the depressive element of her illness was more than just a reaction to feeling unwell. She pointed out that the beta-blockers, while controlling the anxiety symptoms, also seemed to be making her feel worse in other ways. Dr Gregory accepted that this might well be the case but felt that, because the panic attacks were so incapacitating, the medication should be continued in a modified dose. He also explained that he was going to prescribe antidepressants for two reasons: to treat the initial depressive state which he felt was being made worse by the side-effects of the beta-blockers; and to treat the panic attacks themselves. He explained that this had been found to be a very effective form of treatment for this disorder even when there was no depressive element evident.

Sue began her treatment with seroxat, a serotonin uptake inhibitor which has some sedative effects. She found that she could not tolerate the full dose at first and had to build up gradually to one full tablet each day over the next two weeks. During this time both Sue and Mike were disappointed to find that there seemed to be no one available to counsel them about these side-effects, which included 'twitching feet', clouding of concentration and a general lack of energy. Whereas they realized that some of these experiences could be due to the illness itself, they felt that a little less vagueness on the subject from the various experts they contacted, *including the CPN*, would have been useful.

Sue continued with the medication as prescribed for six months, experiencing only moderate relief of her symptoms of depression during this time. The panic attacks did become much less frequent and milder and she was able to return to work with a limited degree of success. Against medical advice, she stopped taking the beta-blockers but continued with the seroxat for a few months more. At the end of this period of time the doctor changed the antidepressant to fluoxetine (Prozac), which has a more uplifting effect. The effect was remarkable and the improvement was very evident within a week or two, although after a further six months the dose had to be increased when Sue reached a plateau. It should be explained at this point that Sue had worked in the same job, as a graphic artist, for twenty years, and for the last five of them had hated every minute of it. Because she was an equal 'bread winner', she was not prepared to take the risk of becoming self-employed; changing to a new employer would not bring the required financial remuneration. Sue felt that her predicament was hopeless, and that there was no alternative way forward for her. The doctor advised that a job change really was necessary if she was ever to regain her normal function and discontinue antidepressant therapy. Meanwhile she doubled the dose of fluoxetine and referred her to a psychologist whose waiting list was at least six months. Fate intervened, and three months later Sue was made redundant. That was six months ago. Today she is earning her share of the family income by working from home as an artist, and is topping up her income with the proceeds from her and Mike's hobby of ceramics. She is far more settled these days, but still cannot recover quickly enough from the kind of stressful life events that are common to most of us – she cannot 'bounce back'. On these occasions she responds to the warnings and takes it easy for a short period of time. She is also waiting to see a psychologist because Sue and her GP feel that she has gone as far as she can on medication, and now needs counselling to enable her to practise stress management. The depressive element of her illness is now under control, however, and in general she maintains fair quality of life.

- Describe physical disorders that will cause a display of symptoms similar to those present in a client suffering from an acute anxiety state (panic attack).

Note: It is important to rule out physical causes before an individual is diagnosed as suffering from panic attacks.

PREMENSTRUAL SYNDROME (PMS)

Nearly all women experience some premenstrual changes and 30–40 per cent think that these cause considerable disruption to their lives (Massil and O'Brien, 1986). For some women the effects of PMS (premenstrual syndrome) are disabling and their quality of life is seriously compromised. Some authorities insist that for a diagnosis of PMS to be made, the woman must be symptom-free for at least one week after menstruation relieves the condition. It should also be severe enough to disrupt normal relationships and/or activities. In the context of this book these criteria would seem reasonable, as the professional health worker would probably not become aware of PMS in a client unless it was severe enough to warrant her asking for advice relating to the problems she was suffering because of it. It is also worth mentioning at this point that untreated postnatal depression can progress to what appears to be PMS. This is probably because a woman who is constantly, even mildly, depressed will feel much worse during the premenstrual phase of her cycle, at a time when, otherwise, she would probably only be feeling the mild symptoms of premenstrual tension common to the majority of women. In this case, careful questioning would reveal that the psychological symptoms of PMS were not only apparent in the premenstrual period, but also through the rest of her cycle, albeit to a lesser degree.

Previous knowledge about the woman's physical and mental health is an important factor to be considered before a diagnosis of this disorder is made because many of the symptoms may have other causes of a psychological or purely physical origin. These include migraine, endometriosis, menopause, thyroid disease, breast cancer, anaemia, ascites, idiopathic oedema, depressive disorders, anxiety states and general unhappiness to name but a few (Massil and O'Brien, 1986). Many women will tell you that they are suffering from PMS because, subconsciously, they feel that PMS is more acceptable to themselves and/or society, as opposed to admitting to a more generalized depressive state. In a similar way, other symptoms can be blamed on PMS; the one that quickly springs to mind is weight gain. (If I had five pounds for every time that I have blamed the time of the month for my most recent five pounds weight gain, I would be a very rich woman!)

However, there is no doubt that the presence of PMS causes many women a great deal of discomfort and unhappiness, and that irritability, aggression and depression are some of the major symptoms. Often problems with relationships bring this condition to the fore. It is not hard to imagine that the damage done in the premenstrual period by an irate/depressed/anxious woman, who could take the rest of the month to put it right again. In some cases relationships can be irreparably damaged. When taking children into consideration we should think carefully about the effects on them. An older child might learn to keep out of the mother's way during certain times of the month and probably will be able to accept simple explanations of her mood disruptions. However, babies and small children cannot be expected to understand why their usually warm mother periodically becomes irritable/tearful/hostile/violent. This situation is also likely to produce guilt feelings in the mother which, if severe enough, could well lead to a loss of self-esteem. It can be seen, then, that this condition, especially when present in the mothers of young children, should always be taken very seriously, and appropriate counselling and treatment should be forthcoming. It is never acceptable to allow a woman to feel that suffering from PMS is just part of a woman's lot in life and to allow the situation to continue without attempts to check it.

Dalton (1969) noted that patients with premenstrual syndrome characteristically have more than one symptom. This multiplicity of symptoms leads to patients being wrongly classed as 'neurotic', just as many sufferers from other endocrine disorders, like myxoedema or Addison's disease, used to be.

Common symptoms

- **Physical**: headaches and migraine, weight gain, abdominal bloating, breast tenderness, backache, skin eruptions, hot flushes, dizziness, rhinitis, sore eyes, food cravings, changes in appetite, changes in libido.
- **Behavioural**: loss of concentration, poor work performance, avoidance of social activities, tendency to accidents, attempted suicide, violent (possibly criminal) behaviour to others.
- **Psychological**: tension, apathy, irritability, depression, mood swings, anxiety, feelings of losing control, weepiness, poor self-esteem, suicidal thoughts, hostile and angry feelings, aching joints.

Aetiology

Several theories have been put forward to explain the reason for PMS, but none have been supported by concrete evidence. It seems likely that it is due to more than one cause. The main theories are listed and discussed below.

1. Abnormalities of sex hormones
    - High blood levels of oestrogen.
    - High ratio of oestrogen to progesterone in blood.
    - Allergic sensitivity to endogenous oestrogen.
    - Direct pharmacological effect of progesterone.
    - Allergic sensitivity to endogenous progesterone.
    - Increased production of prolactin.

2. Water and sodium retention due to
   - Salt-retaining effects of sex hormones.
   - Increased production of the antidiuretic hormones.
   - Increased aldosterone production.
   - Some hypothalamic dysfunction.
   - Increased capillary permeability to protein.

3. Miscellaneous physical theories
   - A specific menotoxin produced in the endometrium.
   - Changes in monoamine oxidase activity.
   - Lowered alveolar carbon dioxide tension.
   - Oestrogen increasing serotonin-receptor sensitivity.
   - Endogenous opioid peptides.
   - Prostaglandin-induced symptoms.

4. Psychological theories
   - It is a neurotic disorder.
   - It stems from early experience about menstruation.

The research done on PMS is exhaustive but conflicting and inconclusive. It would seem that the causes are probably multiple and far-reaching, affecting different women in different ways. In a similar way that the experience of physical pain is highly subjective, but nevertheless very real to each individual suffering from it, surely it is probable that the response to physical changes in the body is also highly subjective to each individual woman. Professionals should always take complaints seriously.

Treatment

PMS can be treated successfully. Some doctors first like to try vitamin B6. If a woman suffers from migraine, asthma or epilepsy, which becomes worse premenstrually, it might be necessary to reduce the medications for these conditions through the rest of the month. Treatment should start three days before the symptoms are about to start, which is usually about ten days before menstruation and continue until about three days after the period has started.

If a woman is thought to be low in progesterone, a progesterone such as Dydrogesterone can be used. This closely resembles natural progesterone and has been found to be successful. Natural progesterone is the favourite treatment for PMS but it cannot be taken orally, but must be administered by injection or suppositories. Bromocryptine has the effect of lowering excessively high levels of prolactin in the blood, but the side-effects can be quite unpleasant. Diuretics may be used to speed up water loss from the body tissues, but this only treats one symptom. The contraceptive pill may be an effective means of treatment for many of the symptoms, but sometimes these women will continue to suffer from depression.

Methods of self-help

Eating well is important for helping certain symptoms. Blood sugar is low premenstrually, so eating small amounts of food regularly will relieve headaches and irritability. Certain foods with high levels of vitamin B6 can be useful, such as liver, eggs and milk, as well as cereals such as wholemeal bread and rice. Certain foods acts as natural diuretics, for example cucumber, celery, parsley and coffee. Water retention can also be aided by limiting salt intake.

Oil of Evening Primrose often provides relief from some of the symptoms of PMS. Primrose oil contains a substance known as gammalinoleic acid (GMA). This is converted by the body into a substance known as prostaglandin E1 which is necessary for hormonal balance. Deficiency in this is thought to be one of the cause of PMS.

Many women find that exercise encourages relaxation, reduces aggression, tension and crying, and the effects of stomach cramp. Applying heat to aches and pains is helpful, as may be a hot bath followed by rest. If a woman finds that she is more prone to acne and skin problems before a period, this can be further demoralizing. She should be encouraged to take particular care of her skin and to seek help from the GP to combat this problem. Acne is no longer something that 'has to be lived with'.

Once PMS is recognized, a woman may find that discussing it with her family may be useful. In this way, the family can work out ways to relieve symptoms, thus avoiding stress during the premenstrual phase. Together with eating a healthy diet, this may go a long way to help her cope each month.

Most clients will benefit from counselling, reassurance, discussion and explanation. For some women, this will be the first time they have been able to discuss their premenstrual feelings and symptoms in any depth. It is important that enough time is set aside to talk properly; it is inappropriate to try to do this during a five-minute appointment in the normal surgery. In cases where problems are being caused within the family, it is probably better if the woman's partner is present, since fuller understanding from this direction may help to reduce escalating misunderstandings and tensions.

In the treatment of PMS it is important that the diagnosis is exact and is based on the timing of symptoms. Treatment should not really start until the symptoms have been evaluated by the use of a daily chart over the period of a month. There is a wide range of treatment which indicates that no single approach is likely to work on its own, so both the GP and the client must be patient and not give up after one or two approaches have less than the desired effect.

- Do you think that PMS would be fully treatable by now if it were a disorder that affected men as much as it does some women?
- Do you think that some GPs should be given a simulated PMS experience before they are let loose on the female population?
- Obviously, this last point is made in a less than serious manner. However, how do you think that you could improve the attitude to PMS within your Primary Health Care Team?

REFERENCES

Bell, R. (1985) *Holy Anorexia.* Chicago: University of Chicago Press.

Brumberg, J.J. (1988) *Fasting Girls.* Cambridge, MA: Harvard University Press.

Dalton, K. (1969) *The Menstrual Cycle.* New York: Pantheon Books.

Groves, P. and Pennell, I. (1995) *The Consumer Guide to Mental Health.* London: HarperCollins.

Massil, H. and O'Brien, P. (1986) 'Premenstrual Syndrome', *British Medical Journal* 293: 1281–9.

Minuchin, S., Roseman, B. and Baker, L. (1978) *Psychosomatic Families: Anorexia Nervosa in Context.* Cambridge, MA: Harvard University Press.

Rapoport, L. (1965) 'The state of crisis: some theoretical considerations', in H.J. Parradox (ed.), *Crisis Intervention: Selected Readings.* New York: Family Service Association of America.

Smith, L. (1987) 'Women and mental health', in J. Orr (ed.), *Women's Health in the Community.* Chichester: Wiley.

Vollrath, M. (ed.) (1992) 'Binge eating and concerns among young adults: results from the Zurich Cohort Study', *British Journal of Psychiatry*, 160: 498–507.

Waller, G. (1991) 'Sexual abuse as a factor in eating disorders', *British Journal of Psychiatry*, 160: 664–71.

Waller, J.V., Kaufman, M.R. and Deutsch, F. (1940) 'Anorexia nervosa, a psychosomatic entity', *Psychosomatic Medicine*, 9: 429–48.

4

THE INCREASED RISK OF DEPRESSIVE ILLNESS IN WOMEN

> Nobody objects to a woman being a good writer or sculptor or geneticist if at the same time she manages to be a good wife, good mother, good looking, good tempered, well groomed and unaggressive. (Leslie M. McIntyre)

CAUSED BY A CRISIS IN IDENTITY?

Weissman and Kierman (1977) have proposed two main pathways by which women's disadvantaged status may lead to clinical depression, but these two hypotheses are found to be somewhat at odds with each other.

The learned helplessness hypothesis concentrates on social conditioning. It suggests that this is brought about by the influences of media, parents and society in general, combining to discourage self-assertion and to encourage stereotypical images. Social expectations encourage these 'femininity values', which are redefined as a variant of 'learned helplessness' which is a characteristic of depression. It is suggested that young girls learn to be helpless during their socialization and develop only a limited response repertoire when under stress.

The social status hypothesis suggests that women are prepared to be assertive and do have expectations but that these are thwarted by real social discrimination. Excellence becomes very difficult to achieve, with a lowering of self-esteem and aspirations resulting from economic and legal helplessness. This may ultimately result in depression.

It seems difficult to accept that both these theories can be correct because the learned helplessness hypothesis suggests that expectations and aspirations are not learned in the first place. If we are to accept that low self-esteem is a major factor in mental illness, it would seem improbable that women who had not been taught to expect anything more than what is fairly easy to achieve, would generally become depressed. The social status hypothesis accepts that high self-value is originally acquired, but ambitions are not allowed to come to full fruition due to social pressures. Here, expectation and achievement are seen to clash, and it is quite easy to see how the result will lead to a perception of failure, leading to the lowering of self-esteem; both seem to be factors in the development of depressive illness.

The fact remains that all relevant research indicates that it is the *married* woman who is at most risk of becoming depressed. Gove and his associates (1973) found that the higher rates for depressive illnesses in women are largely accounted for by married women. Other studies have found that in general practice 85 per cent of patients treated for depression are women, and that most of them are married (67 out of 79). Weissman and Klerman (1977) argue that, in terms of depressive illness, the disadvantages of marriage for women are proof of their theory of *social discrimination*, since the married woman is more likely to embody the traditional stereotyped roles. Gove (1973) draws the very practical conclusion that the real disadvantage of marriage for women is that of *role restriction*. It is not hard to see the logic of this argument, especially concerning women who give up work to have children. Women often expect the role of full-time mother to be fulfilling; society does little to try to convince them otherwise. The boring reality of mixing the third lot of play dough in one week, or listening to yet another theory on the vitamin content of spinach, seems to be a secret well kept by 'the sisterhood'.

■ Is this because mothers feel ashamed of admitting 'failure' in this area?

The majority of women do not become mentally ill. This is attributed to the fact that they show resilience due to a lack of, or only minimal exposure to, the four vulnerability factors identified by Brown and Harris (1978). These events reduce the ability to hold good feelings, due to the experience of loss and hopelessness, which in turn leads to lowered self-esteem. The factors are:

- The presence of three or more dependent children under the age of fourteen.
- A lack of an intimate and confiding marital relationship.

- A lack of paid employment outside the home.
- The loss of a mother before the age of eleven years.

An interesting fact also emerged, relating to the last point: any ensuing mental disturbance is likely to differ according to the reason for the loss of the mother. If this was death, the daughter would experience a sense of abandonment and hopelessness and this would predispose her to psychotic (severe endogenous) depression. If the mother was lost due to separation, the experience would be that of rejection and despair leading to a predisposition to neurotic (exogenous) depression. Considering that there are few women who are strangers to one or more of the vulnerability factors cited here, it is perhaps not surprising that once up against the role restrictions and the socially imposed expectations of motherhood they succumb to depressive disturbance.

Much research has focused on the role of depression in the life of the married woman, although most of it was carried out prior to the current acceptability of the single-parent family. If the predisposing vulnerability factors are applied to the latter group of women, it is both interesting and alarming to note that a majority of these mothers will fall victims to all four of them.

Other predisposing factors are classified as:

- Symptom formation factors, which influence the form and severity of depression, such as age, previous episodes of depression, succession of past losses and subsequent life events.
- Provoking agents (triggers of illness), such as loss of job, a partner having an affair, financial problems, the loss of a child or the loss of a friend.

SELF-ESTEEM

Women can be forgiven for thinking that they are in a 'no win' situation. In our society, to attain a good standard of mothering is considered nothing less than expected. Because the achievements of motherhood are devalued, women seeking approval by developing an appropriately gendered self lose self-esteem by the very act of seeking it. If women try to become more autonomous, they are at risk of being considered selfish and inappropriately masculine. A fine line has to be walked at all times. For instance, it is generally considered fairly normal for a mother to return to work after the birth of her child, but criticism will soon be forthcoming if her career is important enough for her seemingly to relegate the position of her family to second place. This will be so even if she has made perfectly adequate provision for the family during any absences that her work entails. However, it is considered quite normal for the male partner to put his career to the forefront of his priorities. Once at work, a mother will usually be expected to keep the responsibilities and problems of caring for her family separate from commitments to her job; failure to do this will result in spoken or implied criticism of her position in the workforce. Once again men do not find themselves facing this kind of dilemma. It is little wonder that women seem in constant danger of perceiving themselves as failures. They are expected to retain all the qualities of femininity whilst attaining those of the autonomous 'liberated' self. To achieve this balance brings social approval, thus allowing the preservation of self-esteem. The implied failure of achieving anything less reduces self-esteem.

Recreational interests pose similar problems. It would be considered quite normal for the mother of a family to excel at ten-pin bowling, dancing, gymnastics, etc. However, should she venture into the field of bunjee jumping, parachuting or driving racing cars she is likely to be considered irresponsible and less than feminine. Her partner, on the other hand, would be considered to be behaving quite normally despite the fact that he too has responsibilities to his family. To take part in a dangerous sport would be considered a natural expression of his masculinity; approval would be implied and thus his self-esteem reinforced.

Self-esteem, financial status and qualifications

It appears that a woman's current level of qualifications, with the consequent opportunities for a good career and good pay, is very important in the establishment and maintenance of self-esteem in a different way from her other social roles. (Warr and Jackson, 1983). Insecurity is independently related to both the onset of new non-psychotic psychiatric disorders and their non-remission after two and a half years. (Romans *et al.*, 1996). Recent evidence supporting this link has been provided in a study of re-self-evaluation seven years after the original study carried out in the late 1980s. Approximately half of those with low self-evaluation had improved and very few had a lower degree of self-esteem than originally reported. The life changes associated with the improvement were shown to be improved financial security and work status along with improved close relationships. Thus, there seems to be clear evidence that financially secure women feel better about themselves.

Self-esteem and sexual abuse in childhood

It would seem that women who have failed to report childhood sexual abuse are particularly likely to suffer from low self-esteem. The Otago Women's Health Survey of Childhood Sexual Abuse was a two-stage cross-sectional survey, approved by the local Area Health Board ethics committee (Anderson *et al.*, 1993). The sample consisted of 2250 women randomly selected from electoral roles in Dunedin, New Zealand, a university city. Two groups of women were selected from an original questionnaire. Members of the childhood sexual abuse (CSA) group reported experience of some sort of sexual abuse before the age of sixteen.

Method

The abuse was grouped into three levels of intrusiveness: abuse which did not include genital touching; genital contact without penetration; intercourse attempted and completed. The control group was made up of women who reported no abuse either in childhood or adulthood. A two-phase (postal then interview) community study assessed self-esteem and related variables.

Results

Psychosocial variables predicting low self-esteem were the same in both groups, They included 'being a loner', having an over controlling mother, being poorly qualified, giving a history of depressive disorder and displaying current psychiatric disorder. It was found that CSA led to low self-esteem, but only when it was of the most intrusive type. Contrary to expectations, self-esteem was not related to marital status, whether or not she was a mother or the number of children. However, low self-esteem was more evident in the 22 per cent who described their male partners as 'low care–high control', compared to the 12.9 per cent of those who were in better marital relationships. Of the CSA women with poor marital relationships, 33 per cent had low self-esteem. Those with better marital relationships reported low self-esteem in 12.7 per cent of cases (Romans *et al.*, 1996). Mullen had also previously reported that CSA women are more likely to describe their intimate relationships as unsatisfactory (Mullen *et al.*, 1993).

Clinical implications

- Women reporting CSA have a greater expectation that unpleasant things will happen to them and are less sure that they can affect their destiny.
- CSA usually only directly affects a woman's self-esteem when it has included penetration.
- Her childhood personality, her relationship with her mother, her level of qualifications, and adult psychiatric disorders all impinge on an adult woman's self-esteem.

FIFTEEN WAYS TO PERPETUATE LOW SELF-ESTEEM

1. Judge yourself by your actions rather than your inner self.
2. Do not accept full responsibility for your own life.
3. Have clear cut goals for your life but do not pursue them because you procrastinate, are self-indulgent ('now' mentality) and lack self-discipline.
4. Depend on others for 'permission' to get on with your life. Don't think for yourself or make your own decisions.
5. Be a professional 'people pleaser'.
6. Stay in a job which has no meaning for you and gives no meaning to your life.
7. Do not accept that your own growth is your main priority. Subjugate this to serving other people at the expense of your own development.
8. Do not accept that you have done the best that you can at any given time.
9. Harbour self-pity.
10. Destroy yourself with harmful self-criticism and belittle yourself for your mistakes and failures.
11. Depend on others for a sense of self importance. Fail to realize that everyone is of equal worth, including you, and that we only vary in our specific talents and capabilities.
12. Do not explore your talents and capabilities.
13. Do not follow things through to the end. Give up before you have completed a job.

14. Need to prove yourself all the time. Continually compare your achievements to those of others.
15. Allow people to belittle you and put you down.

- I have discussed a report on low-self esteem relating to unreported childhood sexual abuse. What other kinds of abuse are there? What kinds of abuse do you think could result in damage to self-esteem? Discuss the results of any relevant research which you can find yourself.

- To achieve self-esteem in adulthood it is necessary for children to develop a keen sense of self-worth.
  How can parents, and society as a whole, help to achieve this? … Children whose own parents have not achieved this tend to have the odds stacked against them. What resources do you have, in your area, that can help these families? Research and discuss.

REFERENCES

Anderson, J., Martin, J., Mullen, P., *et al.* (1993) 'The prevalence of childhood sexual experiences in a community sample of women.' *Journal of the American Academy of Child and Adolescent Psychiatry*, 32: 911–19.

Brown, G.W. and Harris, T. (1978) *Social Origins of Depression.* London: Tavistock.

Gove, W.E. (1973) 'Sex, marital status and mortality', *American Journal of Psychology*, 79: 98–111.

Mullen, P.E., Martin, J.L., Anderson, J.C., *et al.* (1993) 'Child sexual abuse and mental health in adult life.' *British Journal of Psychiatry*, 163: 733–46.

Romans, S., Martin, J. and Mullen, P. (1996) Women's self esteem: A community study of women who do not report childhood sexual abuse. *British Journal of Psychiatry*, 169: 696–704.

Warr, P. and Jackson, P. (1983) 'Self esteem and unemployment among young workers.' *Le Travail Humain*, 46: 355–66.

Weissman, M.M. and Klerman, G.L. (1977) 'Sex differences and epidemiology of depression', *Archives of General Psychiatry*, 34, 98–111.

5

THE DISADVANTAGED MOTHER

THE LINKS BETWEEN POVERTY AND DEPRESSION

The relationship between mental health status and poverty remains a grossly under-researched field. Lack of data on mental health and income means that we are forced to rely on mental illness data alone. However, it is clear that there are significant differences between social groups: between high and low income groups; men and women; people of different ethnic groups; and the employed and unemployed.

Research has shown positive links between high social class and good mental health (Goldberg and Auxley, 1980; Cox, 1987), but little research has been done to illustrate the relationship between income and mental health. The results of 'The Health and Lifestyle Survey' (Cox, 1987) indicated that men and women of all ages, who lived in low income households had poorer physical and mental health. It has also been found that factors such as money worries and poor housing, appear to fuel depression, causing high rates among women with children (Richman *et al.*, 1982).

For women with children, employment status appears to have an important bearing on mental health. Cox found that mental health was not unduly affected, and sometimes enhanced, when married or cohabiting women went out to work in employment which they found enjoyable and rewarding. Not surprisingly, it was found to be the opposite case if women had to go out to work because of money shortages and they also disliked their jobs. There was also a significant link between health and the availability of appropriate child care facilities (Cox, 1987).

The groups who suffer most from poor mental health, including women with children, are the same people who commonly find themselves living in conditions of poverty. Obviously, there is a higher risk of poverty among people who already have poor mental health but this cannot completely account for the higher numbers of people in poor households who suffer from mental ill health. Studies have highlighted the fact that a woman's social and economic environment influence her mental health status. Many causes are suggested, including low income, children, employment status, gender and ethnicity. It is the interaction of these factors which influences the way in which a person responds to stress. Powerlessness features strongly in the daily experience of these families. Because of their low income, they find it difficult to cope with everyday pressures. Richman *et al.* (1982) studied families with pre-school children. They found that mental health problems among mothers were related to poor housing conditions and housing worries.

LONE MOTHERS

The majority of lone mothers fall into the low income groups. They have poor access to training and to secure, well-paid jobs; often they cannot afford good child care. This makes it difficult for them to improve their lives. Their social life is also limited because of the lack of baby-sitting facilities and the money to go out. When parents from a higher social class have problems getting baby sitters, they are likely to entertain at home. They have the confidence and facilities to do so, and thus maintain social links. They are also more able to afford the travel cost to visit friends and family. Good social support is afforded in the literal sense of the word.

The following information is from a report (Dowler and Calvert, 1995) commissioned by the Rowntree Foundation. The findings were presented by the Gingerbread Group for the Foundation, on the difficulties of setting up home for young mothers:

- No one agency offered all the information and practical assistance needed in the initial days of setting up home. Many mothers learned about the housing benefit system from their peers. Because of their youth, many felt alienated from voluntary groups as they felt 'out of place' among women even a few years older.

- Families could only afford very limited practical support. The circumstances of the birth could mean that emotional support was also lacking. Staying in the family home while awaiting rehousing could also strain relationships and lead to less support being available.
- Young mothers saw the local authority as being the prime provider of housing and knew little about other forms of tenancy. They had difficulty finding suitable housing near their families.
- Many young mothers were dissatisfied with their housing, mainly due to the nature of the neighbourhood rather than the condition of the property. Moving home and improving their standard of living as their needs changed was extremely difficult.
- To furnish a home even to a basic standard, mothers had to turn to credit which they found costly and difficult to repay. Loans from the Social Fund underestimated the cost of setting up or maintaining a home and many mothers did not apply for fear of not being able to cope with the repayments. They did use other forms of credit which have much lower weekly payments but are more expensive in the long run.
- Even small-scale fluctuations in household expenses, such as the need to buy a child's winter clothing, could cause problems and lead to greater use of credit.

The report found that many of the mothers were not given the kind of practical support given to others because the birth of an illegitimate child was not seen as cause for celebration. Emotional support also seemed to be lacking in many cases. For a parent on income support, the present maternity allowance is £100 (1996). The report found that a simple first set of baby clothing bought from the market cost £60. The essential equipment, including a cot, pushchair, bedding and feeding equipment, cost £499 from the basic range at Mothercare. I have checked second-hand prices in the local advertising paper (available in most parts of the country) and the lowest figure for equipment, excluding bottles and teats, comes to £92. For a very young mother, I would expect that she would need much support to buy second-hand items, especially because of peer-group pressure to buy new things.

Weekly income for a single mother and one child (income support and child benefit, excluding housing benefit as at 1996)

16–17 years, living at home	£56.05
16–18 years, living alone	£64.40
18 years, living at home or alone	£73.60

As the above figures make clear, the youngest and most vulnerable women are given the least assistance.

- Look at the situation of a young single woman setting up home and needing to keep herself and her baby.
- What indications are there that she may be predisposed to depressive illness?
- If she is not predisposed at present, what factors may be likely to alter this in the future?
- Do you think that this might be initially negated by an increase in self-esteem created by the fact that she has become 'someone', that is she has become a mother?

Quality foods – such as many cuts of meat and fresh fish, and vegetables which are not in season – are expensive. The skills to use cheaper, nutritious ingredients are not passed down from mother to daughter as automatically as they were in the days when mothers spent much of their time in the kitchen. Another point worth thinking about is that not many teenage girls consider cooking a 'cool' thing to do, even if they do eat health foods such as salad and yoghurts. Vegetarianism is increasingly popular but is only healthy when practised with sufficient understanding of the necessary principles. Correct storage and basic preparation of foods are often not properly understood. Of course this lack of nutritional know-how affects all strata of society, not just the poor. In her book, *Poverty and Health*, Blackburn (1991) reported the following facts:

- Low-income families spend a higher proportion of their total income on food than high-income families.
- Low-income families spend less in money terms than families with higher incomes. This not surprising fact is born out by Ministry of Agriculture, Fisheries and Food (1989) which reported that a family of two adults and three children in the highest income group would spend £9.39 a week per person on a list of basic foods, as opposed to the £5.61 a week per person spent by

those in the lowest income group, covering the same list of foods: milk, cheese, carcass meat, other meat, fish, eggs, fats, sugars, potatoes, fresh vegetables, processed vegetables, fresh and tinned fruit, bread and other cereals, and non-alcoholic drinks.

- Low-income families spend a larger proportion of their food budget on the types of foods recommended by the various food policies as constituting a healthy diet.
- Low-income families shop more efficiently in money and nutrient terms than higher-income families.

Blackburn states that evidence does not support the view that inefficient food buying or irresponsible budgeting is responsible for the unhealthier diet of low-income families and tries to identify other reasons for it. She cites studies (Lang *et al.*, 1984; Calnan, 1988) as indicating that low-income groups have a fairly good knowledge of the value and composition of a healthy diet, similar to levels of knowledge in high-income groups. It is pointed out that even when knowledge and attitudes to healthy eating are positive, factors such as the cost and availability of food may override feelings and influence spending and eating patterns. Many low-income families find that a healthy diet costs more than their budget allows and they are forced to buy cheaper foods with higher fat and sugar content and less fibre. For instance, fatty mince is much cheaper than lean mince; white bread is considerably cheaper than brown bread but usually has less fibre. Unlike other costs, such as fuel, travel to and from school or work, rent or mortgage, and debt payments, the amount that can be spent on food is flexible. Studies show that low-income families cut back on food expenditure when money is short (Lang *et al.*, 1984; Milburn *et al.*, 1987; Graham, 1984).

Another factor appears to be connected with food consumption patterns and the significance of food within the family. Food consumption patterns within the family are strongly related to age and gender. Men eat more food than women (Whichelow, 1987) and tend to prefer 'meat and two veg' (Wilson, 1989; Charles and Kerr, 1987). Women tend to prefer brown bread, fruit and salad (Whichelow, 1987). Children tend to eat more cereal, milk, sweets and biscuits than the adults in the family. They eat more convenience foods such as fish fingers and beefburgers and are the least likely to miss meals when money is short (Burghes, 1980).

In the majority of homes, it is still the woman who shops for and cooks the meals. Several studies have shown that women attach a great deal of significance to the provision of a 'proper' meal (Murcott, 1982). A 'proper' meal in many homes still consists of meat or poultry and two helpings of vegetables; fish fingers and beefburgers are seen as lower status meals. Because meat and chicken are relatively expensive, mothers in low-income families may cut down on other foods to afford just one good meal a day or do without themselves to make sure there is enough for their partner. It is considered acceptable to give the children fishfingers and other foods marketed for them, but they are often not seen as socially acceptable for the working man. Also children's likes and dislikes may indirectly affect the family diet. For many mothers it is better to fill them up on something they like rather than risk refusal when an alternative will be difficult to supply. Low-income families cannot risk accepting healthy eating advice if it means that the alternative foods they buy may be refused. When money is short it will seem more important to buy what people like rather than what is good for them.

The Dowler and Calvert (1995) report for the Rowntree Foundation complements the Blackburn study. This study investigated the nutritional consequences of strategies that lone parents adopt when money is tight and food choice constrained. However careful the poorest lone parents were in budgeting and shopping for food, their nutritional intake was always lower and their diets less healthy. It was found that:

- Poor material circumstances, particularly when combined with severe constraints on disposable income through repayment of debt arrears, are the main factors associated with poor nutrition in lone parents and sometimes in their children. The poorest, most financially stretched lone parents in the study managed tight budgets in several ways, for example by buying stamps for future bills. As food was the most flexible item, this often led to poorer diets, particularly for the parent. Although lone parents who aimed to shop for 'healthy', 'fresh' food did achieve better diets for themselves and their children than those who did not, nevertheless the diets of the poorer families were still less healthy than those of the better-off families.
- Parents who smoked had worse diets than those who did not, but any detrimental effect of smoking on diets was exacerbated in poorer families. However, the diets of smokers; children were hardly affected.

- Ethnicity is an important factor: those who shop for and eat diets that are typical of Black British or Afro-Caribbean families by and large do better nutritionally than those eating meals typical of white families.
- Lone parents seem to protect their children from the worst nutritional effects of poverty. Where there is evidence of nutritional deprivation, it is the parents who tend to suffer.

Significantly, Blackburn (1991, p. 73) states:

> We need to understand the eating patterns of low-income families in light of information about the cost and availability of good quality food. The relationship between food, poverty and health leaves many health professionals feeling powerless because many of the factors which shape food choices are out of our control. We may have to question the value of traditional approaches which aim to change individual behaviour and turn to new approaches that recognise the material constraints of bread line living. Food co-operatives, free or cheap community transport shopping schemes and the provision of community eating facilities, where healthy meals are available at low cost, are examples of initiatives that help families mitigate and deal with the effects of food poverty. Some workers have found that some families have found budget cookery courses useful, although the same courses have also been used to reinforce the belief that poor families simply need to improve their knowledge of healthy food.

DIET AND DEPRESSION: THE LINK?

Due to positive intervention since the Second World War, most extremes of malnutrition are avoided today, even in the poorer families. White bread is fortified with thiamine and nicotinic acid, two of the B vitamins vital for good mental health. Margarine is fortified with vitamin D and milk is rich in calcium and still mercifully cheap. The vitamin B group is made up of several nutrients and many of them are found in the same food groups. Thus, any symptoms of Vitamin B deficiency are likely to be multiple and related to mental health.

Vitamin B12: pernicious anaemia, peripheral neuropathy, depression and mental status changes.

Vitamin B6: depression.
Vitamin B1 (thiamine): irritability, aggressive behaviour.
Vitamin B2 (riboflavin): depression and mood disorders.
Folic acid: pernicious anaemia, dementia, depression and mood changes.

- Look at the food sources for these vitamins and work out some of the causes of deficiency.
- Make a weekly shopping list for a family of two adults and three children with a budget of £50. Include all nutrients necessary for optimum health and energy. You may wish to consider foods such as breakfast cereal, which are fortified with certain nutrients.
- What advice would you give the family about storing and cooking of the foods on your list?

Poverty and diet

The poor have been criticized by politicians, the 'not' poor and health educators for their pattern of eating and have been urged to eat healthier meals. The stress, isolation and depression which result from low income, poor housing or homelessness, and unemployment make the purchase and preparation of food a demanding task. When women are stressed and trying to look after children in an unhealthy environment, healthy eating choices are in danger of being low on their list of priorities. They are also less likely to have access to transport to enable them to shop at supermarkets.

REFERENCES

Blackburn, C. (1991) *Poverty and Health.* Milton Keynes: Open University Press.
Burghes, L. (1980) 'Living from hand to mouth: a study of 65 families living on supplementary benefit', *Poverty Pamphlet no 50.* London: Family Services Unit and Poverty Action Group.
Calnan, M. (1988) 'Food and health: a comparison of beliefs and practice in middle-class and working-class households', in S. Cunningham-Birley and N. McKegary (eds), *Readings in Medical Sociology.* London: Tavistock.
Charles, N. and Kerr, M. (1987) Attitudes towards the feeding and nutrition of young children. Research Report No. 4. London: Health Education Council.

Cox, B.D. (1987) *The Health and Lifestyle Survey.* London: Health Promotion Research Trust.

Dowler, E. and Calvert, C. (1995) *Nutrition and Diet in Lone Parent Families in London.* Findings Social Policy Research, 71. London: Joseph Rowntree Foundation.

Goldberg, D. and Huxley, P. (1980) *Mental Illness in the Community.* London: Tavistock.

Graham, H. (1984) 'Women's poverty and caring', in C. Glendinning and J. Miller (eds), *Women and Poverty in Britain.* Brighton: Wheatsheaf.

Lang, T., Andrews, C. and Bedale, C. (1984) *Jam Tomorrow?* Manchester: Food Policy Unit, Manchester Polytechnic.

Milburn, J., Clark, A. and Smith, F. (1987) Nae Bread. Health Education Department, Argyll and Clyde Health Board.

Murcott, A. (1982) 'Cooking and the cost: a note on the domestic preparation of meals'. In A. Murcott (ed.), *The Sociology of Food and Eating.* Aldershot: Gower.

Richman, N., Stevenson, J. and Graham, P. (1982) *Pre-school to School. A Behavioural Study.* London: Academic Press.

Whichelow, M. (1987) 'Dietary habits' in B.D. Cox (ed.), *The Health and Lifestyle Survey.* London: Health Promotion Research Trust.

Wilson, G. (1989) 'Family food systems, preventative health and dietary change: a policy to increase the health divide?' *Journal of Social Policy,* 18, 2 April.

6

POSTNATAL DEPRESSIVE DISORDERS

Pregnancy and childbirth are major life-changing events. Considering that many women find this transition difficult to achieve without emotional upheaval, it is amazing that so little has been written on the subject. Indeed, this book has been written for that very reason. When my colleagues and I decided to set up a postnatal resource centre in our clinic, we were disturbed to find that the information regarding this subject was so fragmented. It hardly seems surprising that many professionals are unclear in this area when even psychiatric nurses are not properly educated concerning a condition that concerns a potential 50 per cent of the population. One wonders, at the risk of sounding sexist, if the same would apply should it be the other 50 per cent that were at risk! May I quote a close male GP colleague of a friend of mine who made the following statement after it was suggested that the primary health care team use the Edinburgh Postnatal Depression Scale (EPDS) on all their new mothers? He said: 'I am not sure that we would gain anything from this. I mean most of them would show some signs of depression. After all, most mothers get upset when they have just had a baby. It's normal, and it's not as though we can do much about it unless the woman is severely depressed or actually psychotic.' The fact that anything but crisis intervention would be appropriate seemed to escape him, and I do not think that he is alone in this attitude. Needless to say, my friend has since done her best to convert him and I shall be sending him a copy of this book!

To be fair, some women can be just as ignorant on the subject. One health visitor I know wondered if we should put it into a client's head that she (the client) might be depressed when she had previously been coping with her mood swings etc., quite 'happily' on her own. She felt that we may be in danger of 'molly coddling' the mothers into thinking that they were ill when they were simply rather inadequate in their new role. Fortunately, this attitude is rare, as most health visitors, along with the other members of the team, see quality of life as an essential requirement for a happy, thriving family.

If we attempt to minimize a client's symptoms, and tell her that they are 'normal', we are likely to reinforce any guilt that she *will* be feeling about not enjoying her new baby as much as she should. After all, if what she is feeling is normal why can't she cope with these feelings like other mothers? She is likely to stop complaining and simply hide her feelings because to admit them makes her feel inadequate and a 'bad mother'. Let us look at the three types of mood disorder that make up this area of the depressive spectrum – 'the blues', puerperal psychosis and postnatal depression.

'THE BLUES'

Between 50 per cent and 70 per cent of all women experience 'the blues' during the week or so following delivery. It may be due to a dramatic change in hormone levels and may also be a response to the emotional and physical stress of childbirth. The timing of the onset of most puerperal psychosis coincides with the timing of the onset of 'the blues'. This suggests that the same mechanism is responsible for triggering both. The result of the trigger depends on the predisposition of the woman. There are two variations of 'the blues'.

- Type 1. A complete event with no untoward after-effects (in this case we *can* tell the mother that this normal). It usually occurs between the third and tenth day postpartum. The woman often weeps for no apparent reason and feels much better afterwards.
- Type 2. This is potentially more serious as it may be the start of a longer postnatal disturbance. The mother may feel irritable, depressed, tense, confused, anxious and restless. She may experience headaches. The symptoms will occur in different combinations and be of varying severity in different women. It is important that the physician concentrate on the severity of the symptoms rather than waste time trying to decide whether this is 'the blues' or 'true' postnatal depression because this may preclude early intervention and make the mother feel

more isolated and alienated from people who could help. This is likely to exacerbate her symptoms.

PUERPERAL PSYCHOSIS

This disorder is at the other end of the spectrum and its aetiology, like 'the blues', is thought to be mainly biological. Although it is not yet proven, it seems reasonable to believe that an enormous hormonal/physiological upheaval triggers a brain chemical imbalance.

The estimates of prevalence vary between one in 500 and one in 1000 births. One thing that is certain is that the symptoms and effects of this condition are so devastating that it should rarely be missed. However, the severity of puerperal psychosis may be underestimated, especially because the client may have little or no insight into her illness. For instance, she may feel that urges to harm herself or her baby are entirely reasonable and bide her time to achieve this.

Signs and symptoms

The mother will show signs of being out of touch with reality and display bizarre behaviour. She may be silent or talk nonsense; normal conversation is impossible. Often she will appear bewildered and perplexed. Both verbally and physically she may be under- or over-active and her sleeping and eating patterns will usually be disturbed. She may have auditory or visual hallucinations to which she can be seen responding, and delusions may also be present. In 80 per cent of cases the sufferer is likely to show a manic/depressive picture and the other 20 per cent will present as schizophrenic.

Case study: Marie's story

Marie was a 34-year-old, second-time mother who was happily married to Joe. Their other child, Steven was six and the new arrival had been eagerly awaited by the whole family. Marie had experienced one previous episode of depression, just after she was married, and had responded well to antidepressant therapy at that time. After the birth of Steven, she had shown no depressive symptoms and had since enjoyed staying at home and looking after the family.

Marie appeared to be a strong, resourceful woman who enjoyed the challenge of feeding her children well and making sure that they were dressed nicely; she enjoyed occasional days out and special treats. In fact, this woman was a health visitor's ideal client. One Monday, when Michael was about four weeks old, I made my weekly postnatal visit and found Joe and Marie in quite an anxious state. Michael had been crying a lot and over the weekend had been admitted to hospital where no cause could be found. He had been discharged on his normal formula, together with a diagnosis of colic, which his parents had been informed he would 'grow out of'. The baby was asleep during my visit but I was assured that he had cried all night. I recommended that Marie try Infacol to ease the colic, and if this did not work, to discuss with the GP the possibility of soya formula in case of intolerance to cow's milk. I also noticed that Marie seemed agitated and distressed; she complained of being unable to sleep. I suggested that she make an appointment to see the GP and, after talking to both of them for some time, arranged to visit again on the following Wednesday, I left.

During my next visit Marie seemed much better. The Infacol was having only a limited effect but she was reluctant to try soya milk as the doctor at the hospital had not suggested it. However, both Joe and Marie's parents were helping a great deal by taking the children off Marie's hands for short periods of time so that she could rest, and this support had enabled Joe to return to work. The GP had prescribed tricyclic antidepressants for Marie and she felt confident that they would help her to cope better. She smiled as she assured me that she would be fine and thanked me for my support. I arranged to call back the next day. That night Marie could not sleep; at 2 a.m. she went into the kitchen and took every one of her antidepressants and half a bottle of asprin. She then returned to bed and went to sleep. It was only when her laborious breathing woke Joe that he realized that something was wrong and immediately called an ambulance. Marie was very lucky to survive and was admitted from the overdose unit into the psychiatric wing of the local hospital for treatment and observation. On admission Marie was observed to be retarded to the extent of being completely mute. She showed no recognition of anyone and had to have all her personal needs taken care of by the nurses, who even fed her and held the cup to her lips while she drank. Over the next few weeks we saw a gradual improvement and eventually the day arrived when she could go home on weekend leave. The grandmother who had been caring for the children would keep them with her, and Joe and Marie would spend a few hours with the children but go home to their own house for the evening and night. The next day, Sunday, they would spend some more time with the children before Marie returned to hospital after tea. On the Saturday the plan went well and Marie appeared to enjoy herself, playing with the children, feeding the baby and watching television. At tea time she enjoyed her food, laughingly accusing her mother of spoiling her with her favourite meal, and left for home shortly after 6 p.m. She and Joe walked, as it was a lovely summer evening, and on the way Marie told him how pleased she was that she was feeling so well now, and that soon they would all be able to put this terrible time behind them. They had a pleasant evening watching television, retiring to bed at about 10 p.m. Some time during the night Marie went downstairs. Joe, roused by her movements, followed her and found her as she was about to take the full contents of a bottle of Paracetamol. When asked why, she said that she was a bad person, unworthy of the love of her family, and stated that for this reason she had to die.

Over the next few weeks Marie was treated with a different combination of drugs, and eventually had several successful weekend leaves. These progressed to her being allowed to travel by bus to her mother's house, where she spent a few hours each day looking after the baby and playing with Steven before returning to the hospital with Joe after tea. Complete discharge was imminent when one afternoon Marie took the key to her own house and said that she was going to 'pop home' to see that everything was all right and to collect some underwear that Joe could not find for her. On the way she stopped at the local chemist and bought a bottle of asprin. Fortunately, the chemist was aware of her recent history and alerted a close neighbour, who went round to see if Marie was all right. When she could obtain no reply after knocking at the door, she contacted Joe at work who asked her to telephone the police immediately. By the time Joe had rushed home the police had broken down the door and an ambulance had arrived to take Marie to hospital. Once again, she had made a serious attempt at ending her life and this time it would probably have been successful had it not been for the actions of the chemist and the neighbour.

How long this pattern would have continued I do not know, but it is not unusual for puerperal psychosis to be extremely difficult to treat. This time the consultant psychiatrist decided to treat Marie with a course of eight sessions of electric convulsant therapy (ECT). These were carried out on a twice weekly basis. After the third session Marie stated that she had begun to feel more like her old self. Two weeks after the ECT had been completed she was discharged from hospital and has remained well since, although she continued on antidepressants for a year after discharge and was visited by the CPN regularly for several months. I also kept up regular contact, decreasing these visits as Marie's confidence returned. Eventually a normal health visiting pattern was resumed to allow Marie to feel that she was once again in charge of her own life.

- Does your local psychiatric unit have a mother and baby facility where the baby can remain with its mother throughout her stay?
- Would this type of arrangement have been beneficial to Marie and Michael at any time during her stay in hospital? Explain the reasons for your opinions regarding the pros and cons of this. Should it have been possible in this case? Take into account the extra staff necessary to ensure safety for mother and baby, and the manner in which Marie was likely to relate to Michael during certain periods of her illness.

POSTNATAL DEPRESSION

Brice Pitt (1968) found that 11 per cent of 330 women because depressed during the six weeks after delivery. Later studies confirmed that the prevalence was between 10 and 16 per cent. (Cox *et al.*, 1982; Kumar and Robson, 1984; Watson *et al.*, 1984). It was also discovered that many women continue to feel depressed for several months and some still suffer from mood disturbance up to four years later. Women who have become depressed in the postnatal period are more likely to experience further depressive episodes, particularly after subsequent births. The reason for this frequent recurrence is not at all clear. It could be due directly to the original postnatal depressive episode, or there could be a pre-existing vulnerability to mood disorders.

Pitt (1968) made a very useful synopsis of the symptoms of the women he studied. He found that their depression was characterized by: tearfulness, despondency, feelings of inadequacy and an inability to cope (particularly with the baby), self-reproach over not loving or caring enough for the baby, excessive anxiety over the baby, which was not justified by the baby's health. Unusual irritability was also common, sometimes adding to feelings of guilt. Impaired memory and concentration, and undue fatigue and ready exhaustion were frequent, so that mothers could barely deal with their babies, let alone look after the rest of the family and do the housework and shopping. Anorexia was consistently present. Sleep disturbance, over and above that inevitable with a new baby, was reported by one-third of the patients, taking the form of difficulty in getting off to sleep rather than early morning waking.

The main problem for the health professional is recognizing the difference between postnatal depression and the state of fatigue and lack of confidence which is normal in many new mothers. This is one of the reasons that regular postnatal contact is essential, in the home environment wherever possible, so that as a relationship builds up, a true picture of the emotional state of the mother emerges.

Aetiology of postnatal depression

Postnatal mood disorder can be attributed to many causes, remembering that the postnatal period is an emotional one, often fraught with practical and psychological difficulties. To say that this is a period of high stress and great adjustment is probably putting it mildly when we take into consideration the huge upheaval in every area of the lifestyles of the mother and her partner. It is known that several high-stress events at one time may precipitate mental illness and this cannot be ignored when considering the plight of the postpartum mother. She, above all, will probably undergo more changes at one time than she has ever had to adapt to before. Is it surprising that some mothers jut cannot cope? We may look towards poor coping mechanisms in some women (possibly due to the reasons already discussed under general depression) but often postnatal depression will affect a mother with a normally very well-balanced disposition. In her book, *Depression after Childbirth*, Katrina Dalton (1980) explains the theory of hormonal imbalance, which it must be stressed has not been proved. When one looks towards postnatal depression in a previously well-balanced woman, however, it is certainly a theory worth serious consideration.

Hormonal upheaval

The hypothalamus contains the menstrual control centre and also the controlling centres for mood, sleep, weight and day/night rhythm. During postnatal depression the mood, sleep, weight and day/night rhythm are disturbed. The menstrual control centre (menstrual clock) is responsible for the regular timing of ovulation and menstruation, and releases the necessary hormones to achieve this. In pregnancy this controlling function is no longer needed as the control of pregnancy hormones is taken over by the placental–foetal axis, and the menstrual clock enters a temporary dormant phase.

The hypothalamus produces a hormone called *gonadotrophin hormone* which travels to the pituitary gland, causing it to produce the two menstrual hormones, the follicle-stimulating hormone (FSH) and the luteinizing hormone (LH). Both of these pass from the pituitary gland to the ovary via the blood. FSH is responsible for causing one of the immature follicles within the ovary to ripen. It also causes the ovarian cells to produce the hormone oestrogen, which travels to the uterus where it rebuilds the inner lining which was shed with the last menstrual flow. LH causes the ripening follicle to burst and release the egg cell. It also causes the cells from which the follicle has burst to release the hormone progesterone. This hormone is only present from ovulation until menstruation and is known as the pregnancy hormone because it prepares the lining of the uterus for pregnancy. *Oestrogen* is present throughout the whole cycle and has a higher level at ovulation and again at about the 21st day. *Progesterone* only becomes measurable at ovulation and reaches a peak at the 21st day, decreasing sharply afterwards and disappearing with the onset of menstruation. When pregnancy has occurred, the levels of LH, oestrogen and progesterone continue to rise instead of dropping. Also, four new hormones are produced: *human chorionic gonadotrophin*, *human placental lactogen*, *human chorionic thyrotrophin* and *human molar thyrotophin*. Gradually, the placenta takes over the job of producing progesterone and oestrogen, which have previously been produced by the ovaries. Eventually these hormones are produced in massive amounts. The progesterone rises to 30 to 50 times the amounts found at day 21 in the non-pregnant woman.

Other hormone levels are raised in pregnancy and these include *prolactin*, which prepares the mammary glands for lactation, and those produced by the adrenal glands, which means that twice as much corticosteroid is produced. Within hours of birth the hormones drop to insignificant amounts, apart from prolactin, which continues to be produced by the pituitary gland to enable breastfeeding, and by the third day both oestrogen and progesterone have dropped dramatically. During the puerperium, the refractory phase is entered when the pituitary and ovarian response to the usual trigger hormones is ineffective. This phase lasts until the mother stops breastfeeding. If she does not breastfeed, the refractory phase will last for several weeks, during which the prolactin levels in the blood will be raised.

Dalton (1985) took 100 women who had previously suffered from postnatal depression and gave them prophylactic progesterone during their subsequent pregnancy. Just below 10 per cent of the women experienced a recurrence of the depression compared with 68 per cent of the control group who received no progesterone. However, because this was not a double blind trial, we have no way of knowing whether the high success rate was due to a placebo effect.

It is unfortunate that a trial carried out by Van der Meer *et al.* (1984) only included ten women. In this experiment progesterone suppositories were used and compared with the effect of a placebo. The women in question were all suffering from degrees of postnatal depression and no significant difference was found between the effect of the progesterone and the placebo. However it must be said that, apart from the small number of women taking part in this trial, this work differed from Dalton's in that the latter's concentrated on the antenatal period and the effect of the prophylactic use of progesterone as opposed to its role as a treatment.

More recently, work has been carried out to try to find the link, if any, between hormone imbalance and postnatal depression. Blood and urine samples were taken from approximately 173 women at regular intervals from the 34th week of pregnancy until day eight postpartum. The samples were studied for the levels of estradiol, free estriol, progesterone and prolactin. At the end of the study it was found that there was little difference between the samples of the women who had subsequently become depressed and those that had not. The only difference was at 36 weeks gestation and at two days postpartum, when the levels of estradiol were significantly lower. The study concluded that based on evidence, it was not likely that hormonal factors were implicated in postnatal depression.

Prolactin

There is some evidence regarding the implications of prolactin levels in postnatal depression. This could be a time-bomb waiting to explode given the advocacy of breastfeeding by health professionals and others. We have already seen that prolactin levels are elevated with the commencement of lactation. Researchers have found that there is a connection between high prolactin levels and the levels of irritation and hostility. Studies have found that women with normal prolactin levels, both postnatal and non-postpartum, had much lower degrees of hostility than those who were demonstrating higher than normal levels of prolactin. When Bromocryptine was used to lower the level of prolactin, as part of a double blind trial, the women using the placebo reported no significant lowering in hostility. Those using the Bromocryptine showed marked improvement in their mental state, as they became less hostile, less anxious and less depressed. This research was reviewed by Kellner *et al.* (1984); they concluded that nature allowed this to happen to increase the woman's hostility so that she could protect her young.

It would seem that much more research needs to be done in the area of possible hormonal causes of postnatal depression. The research needs to include double blind trials, women experiencing a similar degree of depression to each other, sufficient numbers to give reliable results, and possibly including women suffering from postnatal psychosis as a separate study. In light of the knowledge that neurotransmitters such as serotonin are implicated in depressive states, these also need to be taken into the research remit, along with the total endocrine picture.

■ Why is the theory of high prolactin levels not given a very high profile? Do the health professionals find the idea disturbing, and if so why?

Consider the following scenario. The theory regarding high prolactin levels has been proved and you are advising/counselling a breastfeeding mother who has become depressed. How would you deal with this situation in a way which would allow or encourage breastfeeding to continue?

Before answering this question, take note of the following comments:

- The mother may feel that she has to stop breastfeeding in the knowledge of the information which you have just given to her. Even if this is not the case, her partner may wish her to discontinue and put pressure on her to comply, as his quality of life is also being affected by her irritability and depression.
- The cause of her depression may not be physiological, but entirely psychosocial in origin.
- Many women feel like failures when they cannot breastfeed, Their self-esteem may plummet. We already know that these features can cause or enhance depression.
- At a basic level 'word soon gets round' and it would be very easy for 'breastfeeding causes depression' to become folklore. Years of encouragement to breastfeed could well be negated.

MATERNAL EXHAUSTION

For a woman to be well both physically and mentally she needs to work, relax and have time for herself in appropriate proportions. For the new and sometimes not so new mother this is often impossible. The first few days and nights are made bearable because adrenaline is produced by the excitement of the birth, but it is inevitable that a degree of tiredness will set in. This has to be accepted as normal and allowances made for it. However, sometimes this natural state of weariness progresses to total exhaustion if nothing is done to prevent it. Good antenatal advice, including that given to the father, should help the parents to plan for the few weeks after the delivery and enable them to keep their expectations realistic. Problems can still arise if the baby is unsettled, thus preventing three or four hours continuous sleep at one time. It is accepted that rapid eye movement (REM) periods of sleep are necessary for dreams to occur and that this is important to maintain a good psychological state in any given individual. In World War II, sleep deprivation was used as a method of torture and prisoners were wakened each time REM sleep was about to begin.

If a mother is becoming exhausted despite good antenatal and postnatal advice, or because her support network has gone awry, it is up to the midwife, health visitor or any other professional dealing with her and her family to support her emotionally and give workable advice, which will enable the situation to be remedied as far as possible. If this advice and support is not forthcoming, the mother may well progress to postnatal depression, and in some cases actual psychosis may occur. If you look back to the case history of Marie, lack of sleep was the first in the sequence of events.

REFERENCES

Cox, J.L., Connor, Y. and Kendell, R.E. (1982) 'Prospective study of the psychiatric disorders of childbirth' *British Journal of Psychiatry*, 140: 111–17.

Dalton, K. (1980) *Depression after Childbirth.* London: Oxford University Press.

Kumar, R. and Robson, K.M. (1984) 'A prospective study of emotional disorders in childbearing women', *British Journal of Psychiatry*, 154: 35–47.

Pitt, B. (1968) '"Atypical" depression following childbirth', *British Journal of Psychiatry*, 114: 1325–35.

Watson, J.P., Elliot, S.A., Rugg, A.J. and Brough, D.I. (1984) 'Psychiatric disorder in pregnancy and the first postnatal year', *British Journal of Psychiatry*, 144: 453–62.

7

POSTNATAL DEPRESSION AND MOTHER–INFANT RELATIONSHIPS

In 1991 Lynne Murray and Alan Stein put forward an excellent piece of work regarding the effects of postnatal depression on the mother–infant relationship (Cooper *et al.*, 1991). This chapter is based on parts of their report and on various pieces of research in this field.

All the features of depression are likely to exert an influence on interpersonal relationships, including those between a mother and her infant. These features may include irritability, anxiety, concentration impairments, and depressive moods and thoughts. In many cases, the depression will continue beyond the first year and therefore may still be present at the commencement of a new pregnancy. Usually, the infant's social life is constituted by the mother during the early months, so it is reasonable for us to be concerned with the long-term effects of postnatal depression on the mother–child relationship and the development of the child.

There have been findings of raised levels of psychiatric disturbance, greater insecurity in attachment relationships and impairments in attention and lowered IQ levels in children of mothers who have suffered from postnatal depression (Mcknew *et al.*, 1979; Cox *et al.*, 1987). Williams and Carmichael (1985) studied a poor ethnic community in Australia. Concerning the attitude of the mother towards the child, they found a striking difference between the comments of the primiparous (first-time) mothers and those mothers who already had other children. Two principal patterns emerged concerning the depressed mothers who only had the one child:

- Several mothers reported that, while on the labour ward, they had failed to establish a relationship or routine pattern of management. The difficulties did not improve on returning home, and there were reports of the infant crying persistently, feeding

poorly, sleeping irregularly and only for brief periods, and being difficult to comfort. It is not surprising that the behaviour of the infants themselves appeared to cause depressive symptoms in their mothers who became angry and frustrated with them
- Other mothers reported that the sleeping, crying and feeding difficulties only began after the onset of the depression.

In both cases a vicious cycle was soon established.

When questioning the depressed mothers who had older children in the family, the picture of difficulties concerning infant behaviour was markedly different. These mothers tended to be very protective towards their infants and there was no increase in reports of infant behavioural disturbance. However, several instances of behavioural problems were reported concerning older pre-school siblings.

Zajicek and de Salis (1979) interviewed a group of women who had suffered postnatal depression that was severe enough to impair their daily functioning and relationships, and others whose depression was distressing but not so severe. When the children of the women suffering severe postnatal depression were 27 months old they were reported to be fearful, to have eating problems and to have difficulties in bladder control. Uddenberg and Engleson (1978) found that the four-and-a-half-year-old children of women who had suffered postnatal disturbance were described as troublesome, uncontrollable and prone to temper tantrums.

From studies such as these, Murray and Stein concluded that there was evidence of an increased risk of child behaviour disturbance and difficulties in the mother–child relationship when the mother has suffered a psychiatric disturbance in the months following delivery. However, they urge caution and make the important point that some of these mothers were *depressed at the time of interview* and this may have coloured their perception of their child's behaviour, hence leading to over-reporting of the problems. They also comment that there may be a direct effect of current (depressive) symptoms on child functioning, making it difficult to determine the effect of *postnatal* depression.

Further studies seem to point to the fact that it may not be *postnatal* depressive episodes which detrimentally affect the child in the future, but more *general* depressive episodes. A carefully analysed study was carried out by Ghodsian *et al.* (1984) which looked at the effect of the current mental symptoms of the depressed mother when evaluating the impact on the child when the episode occurred during the first three and a half years after the child's birth. The mothers were psychiatrically assessed at 4, 14, 27 and 42 months and interviewed about their child's behaviour on all but the first occasion. No effects were found of depression occurring in the first four months but there was evidence that depression occurring at fourteen months had an independent effect on later behaviour problems.

Wrate *et al.* (1985) interviewed mothers who participated in a prospective study when their children were three years old. As in the study by Ghodsian *et al.*, again no increase in child behavioural disturbance was found in the children of the mothers who had suffered from a postnatal depressive episode. However, women who had had *mild* depressive symptoms in the postnatal period did report more difficulties. This paradoxical situation seems to have arisen from the fact that these women had shown far greater anxiety about their maternal role and had gone on *later* to have depressive episodes which focused on their anxieties.

Kumar and Robson (1984) carried out a study of depression occurring after childbirth and Caplan *et al.* (1989) followed this up. Currently depressed women with four-year-old children reported more child behavioural difficulties. Reports of difficulties with marital conflict and paternal psychiatric problems seemed to indicate that these disturbed family interactions mediated the association between the depression and the child's behaviour problems. As with the previous studies, no relationship was found between reported child behaviour disturbance and clinical depression occurring during the postnatal period,

It would appear that the association between postnatal depression and later child behaviour problems is associated with family relationships and current depressive symptoms rather than the postnatal depression *per se.*

TWO STUDIES OF OLDER CHILDREN

Cogill *et al.* (1986) examined the cognitive functioning of four-year-old children whose mothers had been depressed during the first year after the birth. These children had scores which were significantly lower on the McCarthy scale for cognitive functioning (see Appendix). The mothers had made a full recovery by the time the children were nineteen months old, so these differences could not account for the current symptoms. Stein *et al.*, (1991) highlights the processes which might account for this lower cognitive functioning. The relationship between the postnatal depression and later mother–child reactions was investigated in this study. Two groups of mothers were used – an index group and control group. The index group consisted of a number of mothers who had suffered from postnatal depression during the first postnatal year. Half of these had recovered by the time the child was nineteen months old. The control group consisted of mothers who had been free from depressive symptoms since the birth of their child. The main significant findings from this study were that, compared with the control group, the depressed mothers interacted less with their children, and contributed less to their children's activity. Their children smiled, vocalized and showed toys to their mothers less during play, and showed greater distress when their mother left the room. In the half of the group who had recovered by the time their children were nineteen months old similar but reduced effects were seen. The index group of mothers had experienced a significantly higher number of marital difficulties and had social problems connected with housing and finance. *Regression analysis showed that it was these difficulties which were the most powerful predictors of the quality of mother–child relationships at nineteen months.* It was considered that a period of separation during the early months and current depressive symptoms made an independent contribution.

Although child behavioural problems would not appear to be connected to episodes of postnatal depression, it would seem that depression in the postpartum period may be associated with less harmonious mother–child relationships and a lowering of the score on cognitive assessment.

REFERENCES

Caplan, H., Cogill, S., Alexandra, H., Robson, K., Katz, R. and Kumar, R. (1989) 'Maternal depression and emotional development of the child', *British Journal of Psychiatry*, 154: 818–23.

Cogill, S., Caplan, H., Alexandra, H., Robson, K. and Kumar, R. (1986) 'Impact of postnatal depression on the cognitive development of the young child', *British Journal of Psychiatry*, 292: 1165–7.

Cooper, P.J., Murray, L. and Stein, A. (1991) 'Postnatal depression', in A. Serva (ed.), *European Handbook of Psychiatry and Mental Health.* Zargosa: Anthropos.

Cox, J.L., Holden, J.M. and Sagovsky, R. (1987) 'Detection of postnatal depression – development of the Edinburgh Postnatal Depression Scale', *British Journal of Psychiatry*, 150: 782–6.

Ghodsian, M., Zajicek, E. and Wolkind, A. (1984) 'A longitudinal study of maternal depression and child behaviour problems', *Journal of Child Psychology and Psychiatry*, 26: 91–109.

McKnew, D.H., Cytryn, L., Efron, A.M., Gershon, E.S. and Bunny, W.E. (1979) 'Offspring of patients with affective disorders', *British Journal of Psychiatry*, 143: 148–52.

Stein, A., Gath, D., Boucher, J., Bond, A., Day, A. and Cooper, P.J. (1991) 'The relationship between postnatal depression and mother–child interactions' *British Journal of Psychiatry*, 158: 46–52.

Uddenberg, N. and Engelson, I. (1978) 'Prognosis of postpartum mental disturbance; a prospective study of primiparous women and their four-year-old children', *Acta Psychiatrica Scandinavica*, 58: 201–12.

Weissman, M. and Paykel, E.S. (1974) *The Depressed Woman: A Study of Social Relationships.* Chicago: University of Chicago Press.

Williams, H. and Carmichael, A. (1985) 'Depression in mothers in a multi-ethnic urban industrial municipality in Melbourne', *Journal of Child Psychology and Psychiatry*, 26: 277–88.

Wrate, R.M., Rooney, A.C., Thomas, P.F. and Cox, J.L. (1985) 'Postnatal depression and child development: a three-year follow-up study', *British Journal of Psychiatry*, 146: 622–7.

Zajicek, E. and de Salis, W. (1979) 'Depression in mothers of young children. Family Research Unit', *Child Abuse and Neglect*, 3: 833–5.

8

SUPPORT FOR POSTNATAL EMOTIONAL WELL-BEING

THE ROLE OF POSTNATAL CARE

In her book *Reactions to Motherhood* (1994), Jean Ball documented the feelings and reactions of 269 women from the last month of pregnancy until six weeks after the birth of the baby. The mothers' reactions were then considered within the context of other research into postnatal depression and the role of support systems. The results of the study showed how the women in the sample reacted to the experience and demands of motherhood, and the way in which those reactions were influenced by the interaction of a number of factors, some of which could be described as fixed, for example *trait anxiety* and *life-stress events*, and some as mainly care factors, which were alterable. This chapter is based on Jean Ball's research.

Six weeks after the birth, 31 of the mothers were showing high levels of *emotional well-being* and *satisfaction with motherhood.* They were very happy and were coping well. One hundred and ninety-four showed moderate but satisfactory levels of *emotional well-being* and were generally coping quite well, although they would have appreciated further help. The remaining 54 were unhappy, overwhelmed, needed more help than they were receiving, and some were depressed. It is very sad that there were more unhappy women in this group than those who were very happy indeed. Even so, Jean Ball wondered why so few (20 per cent) of the sample were unhappy, taking into consideration the loss of control over lifestyle and lack of sleep implicit in looking after a small baby. She came to the conclusion that this had a lot to do with the fact that a new baby generally brings joy and delight to mothers, which more often than not compensates for the upheaval and demands placed upon them. Nearly all the mothers showed moderate (71) to high (190) levels of *satisfaction with motherhood*; the remainder (3) were bordering on depression and showed *low levels of satisfaction*. Thus, out of the 54 mothers who were unhappy (that is, not showing healthy levels of well-being), 51 still felt reasonable levels of satisfaction with motherhood.

Trait anxiety

Trait anxiety and its effects were identified by Tod (1964) and Pitt (1968). Kumar and Robson (1984) found that it did not seem to be a factor when emotional well-being was measured at three months post-delivery, suggesting that its impact seemed to decrease with time. More recent research has found that trait anxiety is often linked to the choice of feeding methods, with more anxious women likely to bottle feed. Trait anxiety was closely linked to the mother's feelings of well-being and confidence.

Personal stresses

The presence or absence of life-stress factors is also found in the results of other studies, especially the stress of marital tension (Brown and Harris, 1978; Paykel *et al.*, 1980; Oakley, 1980; Kumar and Robson, 1984; O'Hara *et al.*, 1983; Stein *et al.*, 1989), and moving house (Paykel *et al.*, 1980). Often little can be done to change these factors, although it is possible that you may be able to dissuade parents from moving house or making any other unnecessary stressful changes. However, becoming a mother is a peak life experience (Erikson, 1963) and a good experience can boost a woman's confidence and self-esteem.

Other factors

There are two groups of factors. Group one comprises the influences linking the mother's feelings after birth, her satisfaction with motherhood and her emotional well-being. As one might expect, it was found that there was a link between the mother's expressed high motivation to motherhood recorded in late pregnancy and very positive feelings after the birth. However, the influence of care factors made a significant difference. For example, those who fed the baby immediately after birth showed much more positive feelings and higher levels of satisfaction with motherhood six weeks later.

The second group of factors reflect the *alterable care factor.* The mother's self-image in feeding and the care factors which influence it do not have any influence over her satisfaction with motherhood, but it does affect her feelings of well-being. This would indicate that the mother's 'coping process' is affected by the presence or absence of care-related stress.

The following factors were found to be most related to different levels of maternal emotional well-being at six weeks post-delivery. The order denotes the cumulative effect of each within the combination shown and the degree to which each factor is predictive of the outcome. If a mother scored badly on all eight factors, she would almost certainly be distressed. Although some of the factors listed (marked with an asterisk) are clearly linked to anxiety, which was a fixed variable, others were affected by care practices which could be changed. Good scores on these factors could counterbalance poor scores on others.

*1. Perception of family support six weeks post-delivery.
*2. Reported self-confidence when she first returned home with the baby (60 per cent on before third day; 23 per cent on 3–7 days; 17 per cent on 7+ days).
3. Rating of her baby's progress as better or worse than average six weeks post-delivery.
4. Self-image in feeding her baby during her stay in hospital.
*5. Perception of family support when the mother first came home with the baby.
*6. Trait anxiety score measured four weeks before birth.
7. Satisfaction with motherhood six weeks after delivery.
*8. Reactions to the atmosphere of the ward during her stay.

These factors show the presence of anxiety as a predisposing factor. It is likely that they reflect the mother's initial degree of confidence, which would affect her level of anxiety, and are then further influenced by the way in which things happen as she begins to cope with the responsibilities of mothering.

The research indicates that it was not the macro-organization of maternity care which directly affected the women's reaction to motherhood. The more subtle care-patterns played a part: the attitudes of the midwives, in the hospital and at home. Both organization and care-patterns were themselves affected by pressure of work and the culture of the hospital.

The adjustment to motherhood, then, is dependent on the balance between several factors. Although the outcome of the coping process is strongly influenced by the mother's predisposition, it is also just as strongly affected by the attitude of family and peers. The way a person reacts to change is the result of the interaction between personal needs and attributes, the volume of stress, and the quality of the supportive environment. (Lazarus, 1969; Caplan, 1969; Caplan and Killelia, 1976; Deriega and Janda, 1978). The result of the studies demonstrated that the supportive environment provided by the midwifery services did indeed make a difference to the interactive framework and its effect upon mothers' emotional well-being and satisfaction with motherhood.

Case study: Janet's story

Janet was a married woman of 29 years and pregnant for the second time. The pregnancy was not planned. Her first child, an eight-year-old boy, had been born by Caesarean section. In her antenatal interview Janet had expressed great fear about the possibility of another section; her anxiety level was very high.

Janet's husband had recently become unemployed and the family was experiencing financial problems and their council flat had been damaged by fire four months previously, but Jane and her husband were told that their flat could not be redecorated for six months. As the new baby was almost due, the couple had done the decorating themselves, but the council had refused to meet the cost; because they claimed that Janet and her husband should have waited for them to do it. This issue had not been resolved by the time the baby was born and the couple had got into arrears with the rent. Janet was allowed to go into normal labour in the hope that she could deliver her baby vaginally, but this did not prove possible. After eight hours of labour she gave birth to another son, Daniel, by Caesarean section under general anaesthetic. The baby's condition at birth was excellent. Janet chose to bottle feed her baby and did not feed him herself until he was over 24 hours old.

Janet's comments on her hospital care

It is difficult to answer about being fit and well because I did feel well really, except that I had terrible trouble with wind. None of the doctors or nurses seemed to know how bad it was; they kept giving me some white stuff which did no good at all. It was only when I couldn't stand it any longer, after two whole days without sleep because of the pain, that they took any notice because I was crying. They gave me some suppositories and they didn't work very well either. In the end I got rid of it myself with experience, bending up and down. The relief was so great I skipped back to bed. Other than that, I felt perfectly well. The only other thing which spoiled my hospital stay was the food – it was awful. I got my husband to bring me some sandwiches because I was starving. And the rules over staying up and watching television. I think they aren't fair at all – they make you feel as though you are in prison or something, saying that you have got to go to bed by a certain time. Hospital is boring enough, so I think you should have something to look forward to even if it is only the late film.

The postnatal ward staff noted that Janet seemed to be distressed about feeding her baby and considered that this was due to discomfort after the section. They noted that she was tearful, not sleeping well, and somewhat irritable.

Janet went home when the baby was seven days old. She wrote about her experiences then:

After I arrived home I did find it difficult to rest, but with the help of my husband and a very good friend who lives round the corner, I seemed to manage. My friend Pauline told me I looked very tired and so that I could sleep she took the baby for a whole day. It was the best sleep I had had for a long time. Don't get me wrong, baby Daniel was very good, but I was conscious that he was there and that I must wake up every four hours for him. I am still nervous now if he sleeps for a long time because I'm frightened of him dying from cot death, and if anything happened to him now I don't know what I would do. The nurses say don't let him sleep more than six hours, and older women I've talked to say let him sleep, he'll wake when he wants to, but I want him up – I'm not taking any chances.

The midwives who came to see me were marvellous, especially the one who came all the time. She used to ask me all about the baby and myself, and seemed really concerned. I really looked forward to her coming for a chat and her advice. She seemed more like a mother to me and always told me off if she found I'd been doing housework. I didn't need to do anything at all, I had more than enough help, but I don't like putting on people.

She discusses how she feels now that Daniel is six weeks old:

In answer to number seven [on the emotional well-being questionnaire] I do get upset easily. I don't know why. My husband says I snap at him for the least little thing but he understands. I also get weepy but mostly when I am on my own.

I talk to the baby all the time. He's gorgeous now he's talking back to me and saying agoo, and he's always smiling. I'd do anything for him when he smiles and tries to talk back to me, he makes me feel all excited.

When my first boy was born, I was 19 years old and my husband was 18. I was very poorly having him and sure that if I ever had to have another section I would kill myself. When I found I was having another one with Daniel, I told my husband to take the baby and leave me because I didn't think I'd live through it, but everything was fine. On my first baby the nurse took all my jewellery off me and put it in a brown envelope. I had bad dreams all during the operation, and I dreamt that my husband came to the hospital and all they gave him was this brown envelope. Yet on this second operation they just covered my jewellery with plaster and I had no bad dreams.

The reason I mentioned our ages is because I think we were too young to have a baby then. My husband never helped me hardly at all. He just didn't seem interested in the baby. Yet this time he feeds the baby and always wakes up when he is crying. And he's even changed him a few times – one thing I thought he would never do. In fact I'm very proud of him. As we've gotten older I think that we've become more settled and not going out doesn't bother us like it did nine years ago.

Sometimes I do feel that the baby doesn't belong to me. It's hard to get used to having a baby really since waiting eight years since my other little boy. After my first baby, when I went for the coil, the doctor asked me if I wanted more babies, and as I really wanted a girl, I said yes. He said that if I had the coil I would probably never conceive again but he didn't say why. Therefore I didn't have the coil and I was poorly on the pill. All that was left was the sheath and that kept busting, and I was frightened as I was told that you had a bad time if you got pregnant that way. I think that had a lot to do with feeling the baby isn't mine, because I thought that I would never have another one. And with a Caesarean one minute he's inside and the next he's out – you don't see him being born – so you don't feel he's yours at first. But both boys look so like their father that I know they're mine and I can see that they're mine.

I know that my baby knows that I love him by the way he looks at me and smiles – his eyes are full of love. If he wakes up crying in his pram and I call his name and go to him, he smiles and gets excited because he knows I love him very much. I love kissing the back of his neck and feeling his bottom. I love when he is in the nude and I can feel his lovely warm body next to mine. His skin feels beautiful.

THE LESSONS FROM JANET'S STORY

When exploring the lessons to be learned from Janet's story, Jean Ball highlights the issues which she considers loaded the dice and made Janet a candidate for emotional stress.

The events of her previous pregnancy and Caesarean section had left Janet with a great fear of repeating the experience. She was convinced that she would die if she had another section, and to make matters worse the pregnancy was unplanned. She had a high degree of trait anxiety and had recently suffered several stressful life events. She did not feed her son until 24 hours after his birth and did not feel relaxed or at home in hospital.

These factors were counteracted by the help and support Janet received from her community midwife, husband and friend. It also helped that her own maturity and that of her husband had grown since the birth of the first child. The obstetrician who cared for Janet was very sympathetic and had encouraged her to attempt a vaginal delivery. When this was not successful, the trust which had been built up between them enabled Janet to face up to the second operation much more positively.

On discharge, her friend Pauline had stepped in at just the right moment and her husband had also been positive and supportive. The support from the community midwife was right for Janet, who saw her as a mother figure.

I found it rather surprising that there was no mention of the health visitor, and concluded that this may have been because the 'hand over' did not occur until 28 days after delivery in the area where Janet lived. Caplan (1969) and Weiss (1976) both define effective support as 'that which enables the stressed individual to accept the helper as an ally, and which assures her that the helper's skill, time and understanding are available for as long as they are needed. The secret of success in being such a helper lies in the relationship which develops between the individual and the care giver'. In Janet's case this obviously worked very well in her relationship with her midwife.

It is important, however, that the health visitor is also there to continue this support, and to develop a new relationship with the mother when the midwife's visits stop. When both are visiting at the same time, it is important that good communications between the midwife and the health visitor are maintained. It is possible that the health visitor will need to build up a trusting relationship with the mother by letting her know that she also may have had doubts when raising her own children, that she has known the odd bout of depression, that she remembers well the sleepless nights and the wearing effect of a sleepless baby. I would now contradict the tutor from my own health visiting days who told us that mothers would not 'look up to us' if we took such a personal, 'unprofessional' approach. I would further suggest that rather than 'look up to us', many mothers would be far more readily helped if they could look 'across at us' instead.

The present thrust is for a key worker to be responsible for the mother and provide continuity of care throughout all stages of pregnancy, labour and the postnatal period (Ball *et al.*, 1992; Department of Health, 1993). The purpose behind this initiative is to reduce fragmentation of maternity care and to enable good relationships to flourish. Jean Ball makes the very important point that it is also important that sensitive care practices are integrated *within the objectives of each aspect of maternity services*, and not restricted to the personal skills and attributes of individual midwives, doctors and other staff.

SELF-IMAGE IN FEEDING THE BABY IN THE FIRST DAYS AFTER BIRTH

The research indicates that self-image in feeding is not related to anxiety, social class, labour, delivery or timing of the first feed for the baby. Neither is it related to the third-day 'blues'. However, it has been shown to influence the emotional well-being of the mother. Younger mothers and women having their first baby show more difficulties in the very early days, as may be expected, but are coping as well as others by the time the baby is six weeks old. A very interesting fact to emerge from Ball's research is that it is the bottle-feeding mothers who struggle more with self-image regarding feeding. There is also a tendency for them to see themselves as second-class citizens in the maternity hospital (Kitzinger, 1979). Ball suggests that these mothers may need more help and support than they are currently receiving and that they should not be considered to need it less than breast-feeding mothers.

The link between emotional well-being, and midwives' recognition of feeding distress, is significant but operates primarily through feelings of self-image. From the comments of the mothers, it was obvious that many of the midwives had provided very helpful and encouraging advice. However, although some mothers were given help, other vulnerable women found themselves locked into a spiral of demoralization.

LACK OF SLEEP IN HOSPITAL

It is easy for staff to forget how difficult it is to sleep in hospital. Many women, who have been in labour during the night, are disturbed by ward routines while sleeping the following day. They are exhausted, but expected to care for the baby during the following night. A record of the need for sleep is rarely seen in the mother's care records. Ball (1994, p. 111) makes the following very relevant comments regarding this issue:

> Part of the solution to this problem lies in arranging for mothers to go home as soon as possible after the birth where they will be disturbed only by their own baby and where they will be able to get extra rest during the daytime. Another is to make sure that women who had a sleepless night, either in labour, caring for a fretful baby, or because of stitches, recovering from a Caesarean section, for instance, are enabled to sleep undisturbed and for as long as possible the following day.
>
> There needs to be a fundamental change in the way wards are run, and in the attitudes of all types of staff and visitors. The mother's sleep is vital if she is to recover from the efforts of labour and the work in caring for her baby.

Ball and Stanley (1984) explored the ways of increasing and improving the sleep of mothers. It was suggested that there should be rest periods when the ward is closed; provision of single rooms for the use of mothers who have had a bad night with the baby, or have been in labour during the night; and mothers should be supplied with 'Do Not Disturb' signs to hang up when they wish. Ball (1994, p. 112) concludes:

> It should be regarded as a cardinal sin to ever wake a sleeping mother . . . and this applies to staff of all grades, but especially to junior doctors doing rounds, midwives, however senior, cleaners who pull the beds out because 'this is their day for doing it', mother's visitors, newspaper sellers etc.

CONFLICTING ADVICE

Conflicting advice has an eroding effect upon self-image and can be made worse by the effects of the lack of sleep that new mothers inevitably experience. Women who complain about conflicting advice while in hospital suffer from lower self-image in feeding six weeks later, and it is disturbing that nearly 40 per cent of the total number of mothers experienced this. The problem has surfaced in many other maternal satisfaction studies (Williams, 1988; Thomson, 1989; Porter and McIntyre, 1989; Murphy-Black, 1994) and has several causes including:

- Fragmentation of care among staff members including midwives, doctors and health visitors.
- Telling mothers what to do instead of listening to how they feel.
- Contradicting the advice of colleagues, thus confusing the mothers.

Regarding the last point, I have only occasionally come across conflicting advice given by midwives and health visitors, but this problem is particularly prevalent when GPs become involved.

Several years ago, I was visiting a first-time mother who had twin boys. She was naturally quite anxious, but generally managing to breastfeed them well. When they were about three weeks old, one of them developed a bout of diarrhoea and vomiting and the GP was called out over the weekend. When I visited, routinely, on the Monday, I learned, to my consternation, that the doctor had told the woman to give plenty of fluids and to stop breastfeeding (in other words 'starve' the baby) until his intestines had settled down. I explained that we no longer thought that it was necessary to take babies off the breast in circumstances such as this, although we still stopped bottlefeeding, and that she should feel easy to start breastfeeding again, which she wanted to do.

The next morning I received a very irate phone call from the GP in question, telling me never to dare countermand his instructions again as I had confused his patient who had turned up at the surgery tearful and confused. Tearful and confused myself by this time (I had only been qualified a short while), I marched up to the surgery and threw myself on the mercy of our very experienced midwife and a younger, more up-to-date woman GP. They put the errant GP in the picture, although I still feel that I could have handled the situation better.

Another time I suspected that a baby had colic and asked the mother to see the GP to make sure that it was nothing more serious. If all was well, I told her what we could do to try and ease the symptoms. As she was distressed I called back the next day to see how she and the baby were going on, and to find out what the doctor had said. When I arrived as planned, the baby was still crying and the mother was not only upset but annoyed as well. She informed me that the doctor had treated her like a neurotic mother and told her that there was nothing wrong with the baby at all. When she mentioned the colic, he said that the baby did not have that either because if he did he would have had diarrhoea and vomiting. He could not see why I (the health visitor) had even suggested it. I told the mother that colic was not connected with diarrhoea or vomiting, and suggested that we should treat the baby as though he had colic anyway. This we did and, the following week, she bounced happily into the well baby clinic with a much more settled baby in her arms. Luckily that GP was a locum whom I have had little to do with since. However, I did put him right about the signs and symptoms of colic.

The point that these two stories make is that while we should not undermine the efforts of our colleagues, we owe it to each other and the clients to be up to date with our knowledge and advise accordingly. We should never put others in a Catch 22 situation, as in the examples which I have just illustrated. If I had said nothing to contradict what the GPs had said, I would have been wrong because the mothers had been given incorrect advice; if I had disagreed with what they had said, I would still have been wrong because we were then entering the area of conflicting advice. On a more positive note, I still have a great deal of respect for another GP, who asked me to write down my weaning advice for her so that she could be sure that she was advising clients in the same way that I was. That is a good example of team work.

The emphasis here is on avoiding *conflicting* advice rather than *different* advice. If midwives, health visitors and doctors start by asking what advice has been given already, they can then build on that, explaining why a new approach may be useful, and thus avoid a good deal of distress and frustration. It is also best if the advice of others is not contradicted unless absolutely essential. On my own behalf, I must say that I have learned to control my facial expressions these days when entering a potential area of conflict.

- Within the Primary Health Care Team:
  - How can conflicting advice be avoided?
  - How can the latest information regarding issues such as colic, sleeping problems and diet be made available to everyone in the team?

REFERENCES

Ball, J. (1994) *Reactions to Motherhood.* Hale: Books for Midwives Press.

Ball, J., Flint, C., Garner, M., Jackson-Baker, A. and Page, L. (1992) *Who's Left Holding the Baby? Making the Most of Midwifery Resources.* Leeds: Nuffield Institute for Health Services Studies, Leeds University.

Ball, J. and Stanley, J. (1984) 'Stress and the mother' (Supplement: RCM Professional Day Papers), *Midwives Chronicle*, 97: 1162.

Brown, G. and Harris T. (1978) *Social Origins of Depression.* London: Tavistock.

Caplan, G. (1969) *An Approach to Community Mental Health.* London: Tavistock.

Caplan, G. and Killellia, M. (eds) (1976) *Support Systems and Mutual Help.* Orlando: Grune and Stratton.

Department of Health (1993) Changing Childbirth. The Report of the Expert Maternity Group. London: HMSO.

Deriega, V.J. and Janda, L.H. (1978) *Personal Adjustment: The Psychology of Everyday Life.* Glenview, IL: General Learning Press.

Erikson, E.H. (1963) *Childhood and Society* (2nd edn). New York: Norton.

Kitzinger, S. (1979) *The Good Birth Guide.* Glasgow: Fontana.

Kumar, R. and Robson, K.M. (1984) 'A prospective study of emotional disorders in childbearing women', *British Journal of Psychiatry*, 144: 35–47.

Lazarus, R.S. (1969) *Patterns of Adjustment and Human Effectiveness.* New York: McGraw Hill.

Murphy-Black, R. (1994) 'Care in the community during the postnatal period', in S. Robinson and A.M. Thomson (eds), *Midwives, Research and Childbirth.* London: Chapman and Hall.

Oakley, A. (1980) *Women Confined.* Oxford: Martin Robertson.

O'Hara, M.W., Rehm, L.P. and Campbell, S.B. (1983) 'Postpartum depression: a role for social network and life stress variables', *Journal of Nervous and Mental Disease*, 171: 336–41.

Paykel, E.S., Emms, E.M., Fletcher, J. and Rossaby, E.S. (1980) 'Life events and social support in puerperal depression', *British Journal of Psychiatry*, 136: 339–46.

Pitt, B. (1968) '"Atypical" depression following childbirth', *British Journal of Psychiatry*, 114: 1325–35.

Porter, M. and McIntyre, S. (1989) 'Psychosocial effectiveness of antenatal and postnatal care', in S. Robinson and A.M. Thomson (eds), *Midwives, Research and Childbirth.* London: Chapman and Hall.

Stein, A., Cooper, P.J., Campbell, E.A., Day, A. and Altham, M.E. (1989) 'Social adversity and perinatal complications: their relation to postnatal depression', *British Journal of Psychiatry*, 298: 1073–4.

Thomson, A. (1989) 'Why don't women breastfeed?', in S. Robinson and A.M. Thomson (eds), *Midwives, Research and Childbirth.* London: Chapman and Hall.

Tod, E.D.M. (1964) 'Puerperal depression: a prospective epidemiology study', *Lancet*, II: 1264.

Weiss, R.S. (1976) 'Transition states and other stressful situations: their nature and programmes for their management', in G. Caplan and M. Killelia, (eds), *Support Systems and Mutual Help.* Orlando: Grune and Stratton.

Williams, S. (1988) Maternity Survey. Ayrshire and Arran Health Board.

9

POSTNATAL DEPRESSION, RELATIONSHIPS AND MEN

In April 1996, Malcolm George presented a paper with this title to the Joint Health Visitors Association (HVA) and The National Childbirth Trust (NCT) Conference titled 'Postnatal Depression: Focus on a Neglected Issue'.

This is a very under-researched area and it is with his kind co-operation that I now include this edited text of the paper which first appeared in the HVA's report of the conference. This version appeared in Mental Health Nursing, *16(6), pp. 16–19, November 1996.*

In contrast to depression as a whole, relatively few research literature references examine depression after the birth of a child. Add the words man, male, husband, spouse, male partner, or father, and the number of references drops to just a few. This is surprising, since across the whole literature on depression the importance of a close supportive relationship with a partner as a buffer against depression is well established. This is as true for postnatal depression as for any reactive depression.

While there is lack of specific knowledge in postnatal depression, there is increasing evidence for a role of interactional mechanisms operating in depressive disorders. Thus, some focus on both partners and their family dynamic might benefit not just men, but also women, children and families.

Research into both depression and relationships has emphasised that, while distress in relationships can result in depression, depression can lead to increased levels of distress in relationships. A consistent association has been found between marital dysfunction and depression. The interactions of a couple where one partner is depressed show greater conflict, tension and negative expressiveness. This potential 'circle of despair' may also be exacerbated by subtle gender differences in the conduct of relationships, and in the impact and consequences of depression for women or men, either as sufferers or as partners.

It is obvious that where relationship distress exists during pregnancy and the birth of a child, it is more likely to compound relationship problems than to abate them. Depressed patients often report that their close relationships were marked by high levels of conflict, or that they perceived their partner to have made excessive demands on them prior to the onset of depression. This suggests that relationship quality should be assessed as a predictor of potential vulnerability for postnatal depression, and that this should include an appraisal of male partners and the interactions between the couple. Clearly an abusive, dysfunctional or otherwise distressed male partner must be considered as a destabilising factor for a woman's mental well-being after childbirth. For instance, unemployment or the threat of unemployment are potentially very destabilising for men, and in such circumstances a mother-to-be may receive inadequate support solely because her partner is depressed and withdrawn. In such cases, some therapy, intervention or advice before childbirth might prevent depression and even greater relationship distress after a birth. Postnatal depression may also occur, however, as a result of external factors, in response to other adverse life events and vulnerability factors, as well as to relationship problems.

SUPPORT SYSTEMS

Two aspects involving male partners can be addressed from the sparse available literature: first, what support might be critical for men to give to their partners; second, how having a partner who is depressed after childbirth may affect a man. While the buffering factor of 'a close supportive partner' may be self-evident, the critical components of support between partners may need to be made more explicit. Being able to exchange confidences and intimacies, and the giving and receiving of emotional support, are some of the most important functions fulfilled by a close relationship. This is true both for men and women, although women are often assumed to be more sensitive to a lack of such closeness than men. It is, however, a mistake to assume that men are invulnerable, and that they never need to disclose or seek emotional support. Male gender role expectations lead to men to deny such vulnerability, but the reality is that for many men their female partner is their sole confidant and source of emotional support.

Research into couples' expectations during pregnancy has explored some of these issues, both for women and their male partners. The results show how, even with the best of intentions, expectations and the fulfilment of those expectations by a partner may not always match. Such research has found that the most important aspect of support for women was that their partners validated their expectations of the support they perceived they might need. They also valued the practical support they received, either from their partners or from others. The most important of the two, however, was that their partners provided them with a form of emotional support. In contrast, their partners saw the practical level of support available as being most important, but were less concerned about receiving emotional support. This difference between female and male expectations is perhaps one that needs to be addressed. In their concern either to provide practical support or to ensure it is available from others, men may fulfil their own expectations, but fail to recognise that, for women, this is not necessarily the most important aspect of support.

It is vital that men understand their partners' needs for emotional as well as practical support. The best practical support, for instance, in the absence of emotional support, may not buffer adequately against postnatal depression. It is also important for men to understand that denying their emotional needs or their own vulnerability during this time, can also be self-defeating. These are considerations that might be pointed out in antenatal education aimed at couples. Men seek advice and information from others before they start to look for other means as coping strategies for their problems and concerns.

GENDERED BEHAVIOUR

Depression can have a considerable impact on a sufferer's partner, irrespective of whether the non-affected partner is male or female. When couples are assessed and one partner is depressed, both partners shown cognitive distortions; this is not the case with couples where neither partner is depressed. Significantly, it has been found that depressed patients interact more negatively with their spouses than with strangers, and both partners experience their interaction with each other as more sad, angry, mistrusting or detached. Living with a depressed partner can be a considerable burden for the non-depressed partner, often with the result that both partners show reduced problem-solving ability.

These effects on a couple's interactions can also be compounded by differences in gendered behaviour. For instance, an important contributing factor to marital satisfaction is the ability of men to negotiate conflict within a heterosexual relationship successfully. Depression, however, not only tends to increase expressions of sadness, but also leads to increased hostility, which may be both inwardly and outwardly directed. In one study it was estimated that there was twice the effect on expressions of hostility as there was on sadness for depressed women. In responding to such hostility, men risk exacerbating their partners' depressive symptoms. If men respond to hostility with hostility or aggression, or withdraw from engaging with their partners' hostility, they may send an ambivalent message: on the one hand they are seen as being supportive; at the same time rejecting. Withdrawal from conflict is perhaps as much of a problem as returned hostility.

Some studies have found that depression in a wife reduces the hostile interactions of the husband, and increases the likelihood of male withdrawal. Withdrawal from conflict is a mode of interaction during relationship conflict which is more male than female, and a pattern that is particularly associated with relationship failure. Set against a background of postnatal depression where a man not only has a depressed partner, but the couple also have a young baby, it is not hard to see that there is fertile ground for increased stress and distress in the couple's relationship for both partners. This could arise solely from the effect of depression on inter-partner interactions.

MEN AND DEPRESSION

Two published studies on postnatal depression have looked at both partners, and another study has been undertaken in Ottawa. In one of the UK studies, mothers suffering from postnatal depression were hospitalised in a mother and baby unit. Subsequent to this hospitalisation, approximately 50 per cent of male partners became clinically depressed. This suggests that these men had been highly stressed coping with their depressed partner and baby, and were themselves further destabilised by the loss of their partners when they were taken into hospital. Anxiety in post-partum fathers has a strong positive correlation with depression. The second UK study found a similar picture, with roughly 40 per cent of the male partners of postnatally depressed women showing depressive symptoms. Such findings in postnatal depression confirm what is known elsewhere; depressive mood induces depressed feelings in others.

Men tend to have smaller support networks of individuals to whom confidences are disclosed than do women. Social expectations of men and male gender roles often preclude men from feeling able to disclose personal concerns, and they may experience rejection if they do admit concerns or weakness to others. Indeed, postnatal depression may well be an area where both male and female partners feel unable to seek outside help because of gender role expectations. Mothers may feel concerned that their competence in child care may be questioned; men do not want to admit they are unable to cope.

Male gender roles place unrealistic social expectations on men: in order to be valued by others (men and women) as a 'man', they must always be seen to cope. This is perhaps especially so where men are expected to be good 'protectors and providers' in relation to pregnancy, mothers and young children. Many men are aware of this constraint, and obedient to it, but it can be oppressive. Men who do not cope or who are depressed are justifiably afraid of being labelled uncaring, unsupportive, selfish, unmanly, pathetic or a wimp. Depression is said to be incongruent with the male gender role, and this emphasises that a 'man' must not even admit to being its victim. Given such weighty social expectations, it is not surprising that couples collude to hide depression, or that men also become destabilised, as these studies have found.

A Canadian study, which is as yet incomplete and unpublished, identifies additional factors which may be important. The study arose out of a chance observation of one of the researchers, Madeline Ryan, who was running a support group for mothers. The spouse of one depressed mother disclosed his concerns at not coping with his partner's illness. Practical support was obviously required to help the family, and the man was also allowed access to information and advice about his wife. Surprisingly, soon after the man started to receive help, his wife recovered. Previous intervention and efforts aimed solely at the mother had proved unsuccessful. This led Madeline Ryan and her colleague Dr Chandrasena to set up a support group for fathers and male partners. Dr Chandrasena identified an incidence of male depression in this group, and found that many of the men had a poor understanding of their partners' illness. The group sessions provide information about depression, and other family and relationship issues are explored. The research aims to see whether a couple-oriented approach to postnatal depression does help speed recovery for mothers.

The department of psychiatry at the Riverside Hospital in Ottawa claims to be the first to provide a men's clinic with therapy and services specifically aimed at men. The high attendance rates contrast with the prevailing ethos that men do not use such services. The clinic's success is based on the rejection of a view which merely pathologises or denigrates men's emotional competence, and a re-appraisal of the way professional interventions are aimed at men.

Researcher Dr Chandrasena has also identified from other groups run for newly separated or divorced men that a significant proportion have children under the age of one. He is interested in further research to determine the role of postnatal depression as it affects either partner in precipitating relationship failure. For instance, some men may leave their partners because they cannot cope with the responsibilities of fulfilling a supportive role. Others, faced with the difficulties of a depressed partner, may use the male strategy of self-distraction to cope. While this can be a productive strategy, often it can also be a destructive one: for instance, men may increase their alcohol consumption, or seek other avenues of withdrawal, such as work.

On the other hand, some women, particularly out of the cognitive disruption associated with depression, may have unrealistic expectations of their partners, which leads them to become intolerant and to precipitate separation. Particularly where men also become depressed, they may be rejected, leading to separation or divorce.

The stereotypical male gender role may be partially to blame. Research into divorce and separation has shown that men wish to be committed, caring fathers, and that committed, caring fathers are more likely to be adversely affected by relationship difficulties, and to suffer mental health consequences.

The importance of research, however, may extend beyond adult men and women. Relationship failure, separation and divorce can often have adverse consequences for children, who as adults may then be more vulnerable to depression, including postnatal depression.

It is significant that men express concern that the arrival of a child (particularly a first child) will adversely alter their relationship with their partners. For instance, some men feel excluded from family interactions after childbirth. Men may feel unable to discuss this concern with their partner while so much attention is being focused on an expected or young baby. Further the impact of such unvoiced, yet felt, male concern may lead to reduced paternal competence. For instance, it has been found that obstetric risks during pregnancy have an effect on subsequent paternal competence, which is mediated via male anxiety or depression. Paternal competence is linked to both male anxiety and depression, and is also highly dependent on maternal validation of a man as a father. Such validation may be lacking in difficult circumstances. By attempting to cope and to fulfil a protector role, men may suppress their own emotional needs and concerns, ultimately to the detriment of themselves and their families.

CONCLUSION

There is a relative lack of knowledge on normal men and male perspectives in relation to postnatal depression. It might be argued that male gender role expectations, operating at both the individual and social level for both men and women, could have contributed, and would predict, this relative exclusion of men from much consideration. Rising rates of male depression and suicide point to a need for a greater awareness of the consequences of family events on men and their mental health. The potential for under-diagnosis of male depression needs to be addressed, and depression in men recognised in relation to childbirth. Such consideration for men would also benefit women, children and families as a whole. It would make men more aware of how to support their female partners during pregnancy, childbirth and beyond.

- Are present expectations of 'the new Man' realistic, idealistic or both? Why?
- How can men be better prepared for early fatherhood?
- How can couples be better prepared for parenthood?
- How could both partners be made more aware of the problems which may beset them after the birth of the baby, and how can they be helped to circumvent these problems by knowing how they are going to support each other and what their roles will be. How can they be helped to make sure that their expectations of themselves and each other are realistic?

10

THE DETECTION OF VULNERABILITY TO DEPRESSION AND THE EDINBURGH POSTNATAL DEPRESSION SCALE

IDENTIFICATION OF WOMEN IN THE ANTENATAL PERIOD

Epidemiological research suggests that it may be possible to identify those at risk of developing postnatal depression before delivery. A cluster of risk factors have been identified as a result of several studies: a poor marital relationship; severe social and economic stress; lack of a close, confiding relationship; evidence of a previous psychiatric history. All of these factors have consistently been found to be associated with ensuing episodes of postnatal depress (O'Hara and Zekosky, 1988; Cooper *et al.* 1988). If a suitable tool for identifying potential sufferers of postnatal depression could be developed for routine use during the antenatal period, it would require considerable extra funding.

IDENTIFICATION OF VULNERABILITY ON THE POSTNATAL WARD

Events following the birth of the infant may play a significant role in the onset of postnatal depression. It is on the postnatal ward that many of the difficulties experienced by the woman who is vulnerable to depression may be noticed for the first time. Staff should be vigilant for the signs before they develop into a full-blown episode of depressive disturbance. These difficulties might include:

(a) *The maternal response to her infant at delivery.* When a mother tells us that her feelings for her new baby are/were not immediate, we are rightly quick to reassure her that, for many women, 'bonding' occurs gradually over a few days rather than as a rush of maternal devotion immediately after birth (Robson and Kumar, 1980). However, research has shown that those who are postnatally depressed are far more likely to have responded negatively to their child at birth. In a study carried out by Murray (1992), 47 per cent of those who had a postnatal depressive episode, compared to 22 per cent of those who did not, experienced feelings after the birth which ranged from ambivalent to strongly negative. This finding remained the same despite any differences in the method of delivery.

The identification of women who react negatively to their babies at birth, if followed up, would need very sensitive management and, clearly, it would not be right to make judgements on a mother's capacity to bond properly with her baby solely on this basis.

(b) *Feeding difficulties.* There is no difference in the number of intended breastfeeding mothers who later become depressed and those who do not. However, among those who do become depressed, the majority of them have given up breastfeeding at eight weeks (Cooper *et al.*, 1988). Some researchers have suggested that postnatal depression may be caused by the hormonal changes involved with the cessation of breastfeeding, but the evidence for this claim is unconvincing. Cooper *et al.*, found that, in the majority of the cases, the onset of full depressive symptoms preceded weaning; this has been supported by Murray's research (1992). It has been found that the feeding difficulties leading up to the cessation of breastfeeding may well play a role in the onset of the depressive episode, in the same way that other difficulties with infant care also contribute. Feeding problems may well begin on the postnatal ward.

(c) *Severe 'blues'.* Several studies have found that a low mood and tearfulness, usually experienced in a mild form about the fourth postnatal day by a large proportion of mothers, are associated with the development of a full-blown depressive episode (Paykel *et al.*, 1980). It is important that these occurrences are noted by ward staff and health visitors.

(d) *Absence of confiding relationships.* Many mothers do not become depressed even though their social history may suggest that they are vulnerable. It seems that these women have close confiding relationships with a partner, parent or friend. The absence of such relationships may well tip the scale against them. Usually midwives will quickly pick up the cues if a relationship appears strained or if there is a noticeable lack of support.

These difficulties often first become apparent on the postnatal ward or during the first days at home. One has to remember that mothers are discharged from the labour ward much earlier than they were even a decade ago. Twenty years ago, in the unit where I worked, it was almost unheard-of for a breastfeeding mother to be discharged before the fourth day because the ward sister firmly believed that mothers needed a lot of support during the stage of 'venous engorgement' on or about the fourth day. Invariably this meant that support was also available if and when the 'baby blues' occurred. Nowadays, support must be given by the community midwife during this period and to enable her to do this, it is important that information from the hospital should be passed on to her. Surely this could be done with the use of a routine 'check list' attached to the discharge sheet?

IMPROVING THE RECOGNITION OF DEPRESSION

A high index of suspicion, improved consultation and the involvement of the entire Primary Health Care Team can provide the basis of screening, both formal and informal. Opportunities for screening the target group include:

- Well-woman clinics.
- Antenatal clinics.
- Postnatal visits.

Specific scales can be used in general practice for formal screening of all patients attending the practice or for at-risk groups or patients where the diagnosis is suspect.

For mothers within the first year of delivery, the Edinburgh Postnatal Depression Scale (EPDS) can be of great use, when used at regular intervals, to check the state of mental health, and I will be looking at this in detail (see also, Appendix 2 and next section). Of the other self-rating scales available, the Hospital Anxiety and Depression Scale (HADS) (see Appendix 2) is among the most widely used. This scale has been validated for use in general practice and may be used for screening, diagnostic purposes, monitoring and outcome purposes. It is specially formulated to detect anxiety as well as depression. Because of its sensitivity and specificity, it can be a very useful tool.

Depression may be common in mothers of young children who have experienced previous episodes of depression, or have been victims of childhood physical or sexual abuse, or have social, family or work-related problems.

THE EDINBURGH POSTNATAL DEPRESSION SCALE (EPDS)

In 1980 the Scottish Home and Health Department approved a grant application by Professor John Cox to enable him, along with a team of colleagues, to develop a questionnaire aimed at detecting depression in postnatal women. His interest in this subject had been aroused by his work in Edinburgh, London and Kampala. In Uganda he carried out a prospective study similar to the one carried out by Brice Pitt (1968).

It had become apparent that the HAD Scale, and others similar to it, were often not suitable for picking up the signs of depression in perinatal and postnatal women. Cox felt that there was an urgent need to develop methods to identify such depression for use in primary health care settings, whether in a developed or developing country. Jenni Holden, a trained psychologist and health visitor, and Ruth Sagovsky, a part-time research registrar in Edinburgh, were invited to join the team, and the development of the EPDS was under way.

The EPDS, a ten-item self-report screening questionnaire, was introduced into clinical practice and research in 1987. It is now used extensively and is regarded with high esteem by those who use it properly. Although the EPDS is a tool designed specifically to detect postnatal depression, it can also be used to screen for depression during pregnancy. However, it will not detect other common psychiatric disorders, such as anxiety states and phobias, or psychotic disorders such as schizophrenia. The EPDS has proved to be a very valuable tool when used in western culture but less so when used with patients from other cultural backgrounds. Therefore care has to be taken when deciding whether to use the questionnaire as a straightforward language translation will sometimes not be enough if the EPDS is to work properly.

Necessary ground work

Before undertaking a detection programme using the EPDS, the ground must be thoroughly prepared. Health Visitors alone cannot be expected to carry the responsibility for such a programme. The delivery and counselling involved with the screening of each postnatal mother within the first six months of childbearing, are likely to increase the workload of the health visitor substantially, and she will need full cooperation from management. In the days of GP fund-holding, it will also be necessary for the purchasers of the service to agree on the provision of this potentially time-consuming 'extra' client service. It will also be essential that all professionals involved be adequately trained and that they are clear about their own professional remit. It is no good if the health visitor, after detecting a moderately depressed woman, then finds that the back-up services are inadequate to help. In some areas this is more likely to be so than in others. Even if she is trained in counselling herself, it is not appropriate that she should be offering counselling at home for anything more than the mildest forms of depression. There should be in motion a system for informing the GP of all clients obtaining a high score on more than two occasions at two-weekly intervals. There needs to be a recognized protocol within the Primary Health Care Team for the use of the EPDS. This will make clear:

- The role of the health visitor.
- The timing and method.
- If any of the routine screenings are to be carried out by someone else, who is this to be and when? For example, this might be the GP if he/she carries out the six-month assessment without the aid of the health visitor, or the practice nurse at the time of the third vaccination if the health visitor has not been able to do a three-month weaning visit.
- The action to be taken when a high score is presented.

When should the EPDS be used?

Optimum times of use need to be clearly thought out if the results of the EPDS are to be meaningful. The original advice

(Cox *et al.*, 1987) was that the EPDS could be given at the postnatal check-up at about six weeks. However, in practice it became apparent that this would not pick up all depressions as individual women differ in the timing of the onset of postnatal depression. Because 50 per cent of the cases of postnatal depression start within the first three months, and 75 per cent by six months (Cooper *et al.*, 1988), it is now advised that three contact times will maximize detection rates. Wherever possible an effort should be made to fit these occasions into the natural visiting pattern of the health visitor. The recommended times are between five and eight weeks, ten and fourteen weeks and 20 and 26 weeks.

At between five and eight weeks high scores may be a result of the mother still adjusting to the baby, and the mother may only need information and reassurance. Intervention in the form of listening and support may prevent long-lasting depression. Low-scoring women may become depressed later, so all women should be asked to complete a second EPDS at between ten and fourteen weeks. A third EPDS given at between 20 and 26 weeks will detect persistent or late onset depression.

It is useful if some explanation of the EPDS and the way it works can be given during pregnancy; some teams may ask the midwife to take responsibility for this. If the health visitor carries out routine antenatal visits, she may feel that she prefers to do this herself. Either way, the role of the health professionals should be properly explained at the same time. It is also useful if the information is given to both prospective parents. Discuss possible emotional responses, including low moods, depression and maternal exhaustion. At this stage it may be appropriate to encourage plans to avoid exhaustion by enlisting help and support for the early postnatal weeks.

Contact times

These should be chosen to fit in with the times mothers are routinely seen, such as postnatal visits, weaning visits and developmental assessments. If the mother is seen at clinic, adequate privacy should be ensured. However, do not rely on clinics for this purpose, as non-attenders may well be depressed. It is also quite common that the mother will use the EPDS as permission to talk and for this reason I much prefer the home visit at a suitable time for discussing this issue. However, some workloads may not allow this luxury.

Completing the EPDS

The EPDS only takes a few minutes to complete. It should be filled in by the woman herself, without help from other people. Make sure that all items have been completed. Discreet help may be offered if the woman has literacy problems.

Scoring

The EPDS items are scored on a scale of 0–3; the normal response scores 0, and the 'severe' response scores 3. Total the individual item scores.

Action

Women who score 12 or more on the EPDS should be seen by a health professional as soon as possible for discussion and assessment. Anyone who scores on item 10 (especially with a high overall score) should be seen and assessed by a doctor as soon as possible. In *Perinatal Psychiatry* (Cox and Holden, 1994), Jenni Holden reports that some health visitors have expressed concern that they cannot look at the results until the following day when the EPDS has been given out at a busy clinic. They are worried about what might happen in the intervening 24 hours should the client have scored highly on the self-harm item (item 10). Holden goes on to give excellent advice on what to do in this case:

> If the EPDS is given at a busy clinic, it is important to scan the completed forms to quickly identify high-scoring women and especially for high-scoring responses on item 10. When combined with a high overall score the women should be seen as soon as possible, and their doctor informed. Ideally, this should not be done without the women's consent. If, however, the health professional knows that she/he will not be able to see the women within 48 hours (for example, if the clinic was on a late Friday afternoon), the doctor should be told and asked to visit.

Holden then goes on to suggest areas to discuss when talking to women who score high on item 10:

1. How often and how severe is the feeling?
2. Has she made any previous attempt?
3. Has she thought how she should go about it?

4. Has she got the means? (And are these likely to be effective?)
5. What has she got to live for?
6. What support does she have at home?
7. If she has a partner, has she told him how she is feeling?
8. Can she count on him to understand and give her emotional support?
9. If she hasn't told him, would she like you or her doctor to explain how she is feeling?
10. If she doesn't have a partner or feels that she really can't tell him, is there anyone else who would be understanding (not judgemental) and whose support she could realistically call on?
11. Has she told this person or anyone else about her feelings?
12. Could she telephone this person and would he/she come if she feels bad?
13. Do her parents know? (Is she close to them?)

Let the woman know it is important to seek help, and that help is available. If you are not her doctor, try to persuade her that you can tell her doctor how she is feeling and ask her or him to call. Although it is necessary to assess the risk and the availability of support, this should not be an interrogation. Encourage the woman to talk in her own way.

- Try role playing a situation where you are the health professional presenting the scale and your partner is the mother in question. Your remit is to talk her through a high score on item 10 and an overall score of 15.

A REPORT ON A PILOT PROJECT TO IDENTIFY POSTNATAL DEPRESSION

This project was implemented by a group of health visitors in Sevenoaks, Kent, to test a structured approach to detecting postnatal depression in its early stages, in order to be able to offer appropriate intervention. The project was intended to assess the value to mothers and usefulness to the health visiting service of using the EPDS to identify postnatal depression. Meetings were held with the local health visitors and managers to discuss participation. Six health visitors agreed to use the questionnaire with their clients, with two to act as controls.

The health visitors using the EPDS sent a letter explaining the project to all new mothers of new births during the three-month trial period. They also gave them the EPDS questionnaire and asked them to complete it, either at a clinic or during a home visit. The questionnaires were then scored and the results discussed with the mothers, and their partners if possible. Women with scores of ten or more were offered further counselling; those with scores of more than twelve were also offered a referral if the health visitor and the client considered it appropriate. Women with high scores were asked to complete the questionnaire again after four to six weeks. At the end of the three-month period, the health visitors who used the EPDS completed an open-ended questionnaire.

During the study, 88 new births were recorded on the eight health visitors' caseloads, and 56 mothers completed the EPDS. Nine mothers had scores of 12 or above (16 per cent). None of the clients who were not offered the EPDS were identified as being postnatally depressed. Eight of the nine clients identified with postnatal depression (PND) were detected at ten to twelve weeks following the birth; one was given the EPDS to complete at four weeks because the health visitor was very concerned about her. In six of the nine cases the findings were totally unexpected.

Subsequent to the assessment, one mother was offered weekly visits by her health visitor, and the other eight received fortnightly visits. Two clients were also referred to the GP. When the EPDS was repeated four to six weeks later, following health visitor intervention, the scores of six of the nine women were found to have dropped to below ten; one scored ten, but had recently started a new job; one had only recently been diagnosed as being depressed. The other had left the area.

All six health visitors completed the open-ended questionnaire. They agreed that postnatal depression is a highly relevant issue for health visitors. Five of the six thought that the EPDS was a useful tool to identify PND. One health visitor, with a very high caseload, said that she had more important priorities to deal with, before those concerning postnatal depression. The health visitors made suggestions for additional questions to be asked, covering issues such as eating habits, appetite, irritability, early feelings towards the baby, and relationships with partners. Two health visitors suggested that questions should be asked to discover how clients were coping with everyday activities such as housework. One health visitor said that she would have liked the

EPDS to give an idea of the client's perception of PND, and whether friends and family had any knowledge or experience of it.

All the health visitors said that some clients would not have been identified without use of the EPDS, referring to the fact that six of the nine high-scoring mothers were unexpected. It was agreed that ten weeks was the best time to use the scale and that the mothers, if not for the EPDS, would not have received a visit at this time. Several of the health visitors who visited fortnightly after identification of postnatal depression would have preferred to visit weekly but were unable to do so due to lack of time. All of the health visitors felt competent in identifying PND but requested further training, especially in updating and developing counselling skills. All six, including the one with the high caseload, said that they wanted to continue to use the scale.

The study showed that:

- The EPDS is a useful tool for health visitors to use to identify postnatal depression, and can usually be incorporated into their routine workload.
- The structured approach is appropriate to health visitors and accepted by clients.
- Incidence of PND is significantly high in the population in general, and may be higher than indicated by previous research.

Other issues for the health-visiting service raised by the study findings were:

- The possible need for further questions to be added to the questionnaire.
- The need for health visitors to receive in-service training to improve counselling skills.
- The importance of home visits and the health visitor's relationship with the family. The issue of home visits further raised the question of resources, as it was felt that the clinic was not an appropriate venue for the completion of the EPDS.

Author's comments

A number of issues concerned me when reading this report:

- Visits every two weeks are probably not frequent enough when counselling a mother with an EPDS score of ten or more. If the health visitor cannot see her more often than this, someone else on the Primary Health Care Team should take on the counselling role.
- I do feel that the health visitors should have been fully updated in counselling skills *before* they were asked to take part in this study. In the report it is stated that most of the women scoring twelve had scores of less than ten on repeating the scale a month or so later. I am interested to know what these second scores were and if they were *significantly* less than ten. If not, I would suggest that the counselling might have been more successful if the health visitors had been better prepared.
- There is very little mention of GP referral in the report and *none at all* for mothers who scored below twelve. Health visitors may sometimes take on a great deal of responsibility without the necessary counselling experience to support it. Obviously, mothers have to agree to see their GP, and it may not be necessary in all cases. This is where the health visitor's sound knowledge of postnatal depressive illness allows her to encourage appropriate explanations regarding a possible biological/hormonal imbalance so that, should any medical intervention be necessary, the mother will accept it.

REFERENCES

Cooper, P.J., Campbell, E.A., Day, A., Kennerly, H. and Bond, A. (1988) 'Non-psychotic disorder after childbirth: a prospective study of prevalence, incidence, course and nature', *British Journal of Psychiatry*, 152: 799–806.

Cox, J.L. and Holden, J. (1994) *Perinatal Psychiatry: Use and Misuse of the Edinburgh Postnatal Depression Scale*. Glasgow: Bell & Bain.

Cox, J.L., Holden, J. and Sagovsky, R. (1987) 'Detection of postnatal depression: development of the ten item Edinburgh Postnatal Depression Scale', *British Journal of Psychiatry*, 150: 111–17.

O'Hara, M.W. and Zekosky, E.M. (1988) 'Postpartum depression: a comprehensive review', in R. Kumar and I.F. Brockington (eds), *Motherhood and Mental Illness*. London: John Wright.

Murray, L. (1992) 'The impact of postnatal depression on infant development', *Journal of Child Psychology*, 33: 543–61.

Paykel, E.S., Emms, E.M., Fletcher, J. and Rossaby, E.S. (1980) 'Life events and social support in puerperal depression', *British Journal of Psychiatry*, 136: 339–46.

Pitt, B. (1968) 'Atypical depression following childbirth', *British Journal of Psychiatry*, 114: 1325–35.

11

WHY DEPRESSION IS MISSED

It is estimated that up to 50 per cent of cases of depression are unrecognized and untreated. Up to 70 per cent of the 4,000 people who commit suicide each year were depressed before they killed themselves. Depression can be missed in general practice and in the community through factors associated with the health care professional, the setting or the client herself. In the following chapters I would like to look at the reasons for this.

- Before you read on, list the reasons why you think depression can be missed.

THE REASONS FOR MISSING DEPRESSION

General Practitioner

The GP may be reluctant to make the diagnosis. Depression is sometimes associated with patients who attend surgery frequently with varying complaints which are time-consuming and never appear to be satisfactorily dealt with. Sometimes mothers of babies and/or young children continuously present their children with relatively minor complaints or management problems. These patients may mislead the doctor because their complaints are somatic, and present as physical disorders. In such cases, GPs need to maintain a high index of suspicion for depression.

In general practice the consultation process is sometimes less than desirable because of the pressure on surgery time, and the fact that the patient may see a different GP on each visit. This makes it difficult to recognize the subtleties of a patient's ongoing problems.

Patient

The patient may be afraid of appearing weak or 'tainted' with mental illness. Because she wants to avoid what she perceives as a stigma, she is reluctant to tell her GP how she feels. On the other hand, the patient may accept that she is depressed, but see this as a normal response to difficult circumstances in her life. In such a case, the patient is unlikely to take her problem to the GP.

Midwife

The midwife is likely to be the first person to recognize symptoms of depression after childbirth. However, the midwife may miss diagnosis when she did not know the mother in the antenatal period, that is at the parentcraft classes. She cannot be expected to notice personality change as readily as a midwife who has come to know the client well in the period before the birth. It is also harder to spot symptoms when various midwives have visited the mother in the postnatal period. This does not allow a relationship to develop or allow the midwife to form a true picture of her client's mental state. The midwife can easily be misled by the client who covers up her mental state or convincingly puts her tears down to 'just the blues'. Relatives may collude with this if they are frightened that they will be seen not to be coping.

The patient may not be able to express how she feels. This is particularly so for women from different cultural backgrounds where no words for depression exist. These patients may only be able to describe how they feel in terms of physical symptoms.

The mother may be frightened of her own feelings, so need to deny them or brush them aside. She may also be ashamed to admit that she does not come up to her own expectations of the 'perfect mother'. She may feel that she has no right to feel anything other than happy when she has a healthy baby. The mother may not wish to admit how she feels for fear of being thought to be 'mad' or unable to cope with her child. Or she may not want to discuss her feelings when other people are present. It is important that she be given the opportunity for private conversations.

Health visitor

The health visitor may have problems identifying symptoms of depression for much the same reasons as the midwife, but because she is involved for a much longer period of time other factors may also be present. Because of work overload she may have to be selective in whom she visits for any length of time. It is important that the client is seen regularly for the first six weeks and then again at three months. Extra visits must be arranged as necessary. Many health visitors cannot do this due to staff shortages, excessive numbers of families with social problems, etc. As a result, postnatal depression can be missed. Although the same health visitor may see the client and her baby regularly in clinic, this is not the ideal place to notice whether or not the mother is experiencing problems. It is important that the health visitor is very aware of voice tone, body language and facial expression when seeing a new mother mainly in the clinic environment. A good liaison system also should be in place when the clinic health visitor is not the client's named health visitor.

Even when the health visitor does pick up signs of depression, it may be difficult to counsel the mother if a good relationship has not been formed in the early weeks, either through lack of visiting time or a change of health visitor. In addition, the health visitor may not feel that she is able to cope with counselling for emotional problems and may subconsciously avoid the issue. Regular use of the Edinburgh Postnatal Depression Scale would help to avoid this, especially if health visitors are properly trained.

The patient may feel that she cannot talk to the health visitor because she does not know her very well. She may not have the confidence to bring the subject up unless she is prompted. Or, she may not see that it is relevant to discuss her emotional problems with the health visitor, whom she may perceive as an authoritarian figure who is only interested in seeing that the children are well cared for.

The mother may feel that the health visitor is too busy to spend time with her on a regular basis. Remember that guilt is often part of the depressive picture and the mother may well feel that she should not waste the time of people 'who have more important things to do'. She may not like her health visitor, or feel that the health visitor does not like her, or disapproves of the way she looks after her child. Any probing may be considered as either veiled or direct criticism. The mother may have been brought up to be suspicious or resentful of people who tell you how to look after your children. This attitude is not restricted to any one social class.

The mother may not want to admit to the health visitor how bad things are because she feels that she is a bad mother and wife, and does not realize herself that her problems are caused by depression. She only recognizes her often inappropriate response to situations, for example, shouting at the baby when he/she cries, her lack of libido, her lack of concentration. She may come to see these features as a 'normal' part of her personality, especially if she has been depressed for some time. It may take a crisis before she will contact her health visitor.

It is apparent that the reasons for missed and mis-diagnosis are manifold. Paykel and Priest (1992) suggest that it would be helpful for GPs to be trained to improve their interviewing skills. The method shown to be of most value in improving recognition is using video feed back in a one-to-one or group setting. GPs can then be trained to teach their own trainees the relevant techniques. Training of health visitors is already taking place in several areas and the use of tools such as the Edinburgh Postnatal Depression Scale is proving worthwhile. It is also valuable in group practices, if continuity of contact is assured and patients can always see their own doctor.

> Many of the issues in improving recognition of depression are educational. These include not only education of general practitioners but in undergraduate medical education and training of doctors in the pre-registration and senior house officer years. Public education is also important to reduce stigma, encourage acknowledgment of depression to the doctor and to allow self recognition by families. (Paykel and Priest, 1992, p. 1202)

REFERENCES

Paykel, E.S. and Priest, R.G. (1992) 'Recognition and management of depression in general practice: consensus statement', *British Medical Journal*, 305, p. 1199.

12

A MULTIDISCIPLINARY APPROACH TO DETECTION AND MANAGEMENT

The management of depression should be a joint effort. All members of the Primary Health Care Team can play important roles in helping to detect and defeat depression. These include the doctor, psychologist, practice nurse, community psychiatric nurse (CPN), health visitor, midwife, district nurse and receptionist. If they maintain a high level of awareness, they can improve the detection rate of depressive illness and help the patient to accept treatment more readily. In order to do this, it will be necessary to hold regular multidisciplinary practice meetings dealing with mental health.

To be effective, a system must be set up to pass on information to all members of the Primary Health Care Team. Information can be given at staff meetings, special identification lists and reports can be placed in patients' notes, special stickers can be put on notes. Confidentiality should not be a problem if everyone is open and honest. Obviously, it would be out of place for a receptionist to tell a patient that she may be suffering from depression, but in the majority of cases other members of the team should be able to approach the problem in an open way. It is important that public awareness is raised and this can be helped by placing leaflets and posters in the waiting areas. Health visitors can also help raise awareness by using the EPDS to monitor postnatal depression in all clients, and use this as an opportunity to discuss the condition. A mother who is not depressed can still be of great help in supporting a relative or friend with a similar condition.

COMMUNICATION SKILLS

When depression is suspected, good communication skills during a consultation can help a mother feel that she is understood and will also help the members of the team to recognize any mental disorder.

Appropriate body language

Speaking involves much more than the language you use. Your entire body reinforces or subverts what you are saying. Your body, your expression and your gestures will create a total impression. Non-verbal messages either reinforce or cancel out what you are trying to say. For instance, if a client notices you looking at your watch during a consultation, she will immediately think that you feel that she is taking up too much of your time. This is why counsellors often give appointments for a set length of time; the client then knows that the time allocation belongs to her and she need not feel guilty using it.

It is also important to note your client's body language as well as conveying positive messages yourself.

- Take into account the points below and try to decide what kind of body language would imply that a person did or did not like you and was or was not listening to you. What body language would indicate shock or acceptance about what was being said?
  - posture
  - mouth/jaw
  - proximity/distance
  - eye contact
  - voice
  - appearance

The client should be allowed to talk to you without interruption unless it is appropriate to do so. However, it is important that you ask questions in relation to what the client has said. The questions should be open, rather than closed. You can then follow up with direct questions as appropriate:

Open questions
Tell me how you are feeling.
Why do you think that you cry so easily?

When did you last cry for no real reason?
Are you waking in the early hours of the morning?
Closed questions
I suppose that your husband has been upsetting you?
You are feeling as bad as last time, aren't you?

Avoid bland reassurances. A client does not want or need to be told 'you'll be fine' or 'It's not as bad as you think' when she feels that her whole world is falling apart. It is important that you are willing to discuss emotional, psychological and social issues as well as her or her child's physical symptoms or problems. When patients have presented with somatic problems, and the diagnosis of depression is confirmed, the GP will need to ensure that the patient accepts this diagnosis. This can be harder than you would think, as some people react with chagrin to the idea that their physical symptoms are being 'dismissed' as a depressive illness. Often they will appear to accept what the GP says and then fail to comply with treatment, especially if that treatment causes any side effects. Treatment is much more likely to succeed if the patient is gently led to recognize the link between the mind's perception of pain and their emotional state. It is not sufficient to state that there is no physical cause for the pain – this will alienate the patient. Sometimes she will accept terms such as 'stress', 'anxiety' and 'tension'. In such cases some GPs have found it helpful to explain that there is evidence that antidepressant medication and counselling also help with this kind of illness. If the patient knows this, she is more likely to undertake the therapy and will not feel fobbed off if antidepressants are prescribed. When the diagnosis of depression is offered it is important to check what the patient understands this term to mean. She may have a different idea of its meaning and significance.

Once the doctor has assessed the degree of depression he or she will then decide what to do next. A number of options are available, including counselling, referral to a psychologist, medication, or in severe cases referral on to a psychiatrist. He will arrange to see the patient on a regular basis to monitor the situation and in nearly all cases other members of the PHCT will now become involved (or continue their initial involvement and liaising with the GP). The roles of these team members are discussed in the next section.

- Think of your relationship with your own GP. Could you speak easily to her or him regarding emotional problems? If not, why not? If you could, what made her or him such a good listener?

WHO CAN DO WHAT?

General practitioners

Before treating the depression, the doctor will need to know how severe it is. If he/she has used the HAD or Edinburgh Scales, he/she will know quite well, but may also wish to consider the degree of social impairment the situation is causing. For example, the mother may be able to cope quite well with her family, but may be having difficulties at work due to the fact that she is not sleeping well. Conversely, she may appear to the outside world to be coping well, but she may be unable to do the shopping or housework. Some new mothers suffering from postnatal depression find that they can care very well for the baby, but only to the total exclusion of everything else. The GP will need to monitor progress in these areas during subsequent visits and often the midwife, health visitor or practice nurse can be very useful in helping to do this.

An essential aspect of the GPs role is to assess the risk of suicide. An important initial step in the management of even mild depression is the identification of potential suicides. Although it is difficult to identify the patients most at risk, the following factors should be taken into serious consideration:

- A recent suicide attempt.
- Persistent suicidal thoughts.
- Persistent hopelessness/pessimism.

Some doctors find it useful to de-mystify suicide, and give the patient permission to feel the way she does.

For example: 'You do seem depressed, and sometimes depression makes you feel that life is not worth living. Have you felt that way? Have you ever thought of doing anything about it?'

Sensitive but clear, direct questions may be appropriate, such as:
'Do you ever feel that life is not worth living?' or
'Have you ever thought of harming yourself?'

Hopelessness is also a good marker:

'Does life ever seem hopeless or pointless?' or
'Do you ever wish that you did not have to wake up in the morning?'

Other ways of broaching the subject include asking about future plans:

'Do you have any plans for the future?' or
'What are you going to do when you are over this?'

Some form of suicide assessment should always be included in the notes of severely depressed patients. Patients who give suicide warnings should always be taken seriously.

A significant number of patients will use their prescribed antidepressant as a means of attempting suicide. Because several antidepressants will make the patient feel worse before she feels better, it is useful to know the relative risk from overdose for each type. When there is concern about possible suicide risk, it is wiser to prescribe an antidepressant that is relatively less toxic in overdose. Table 1 shows the relative risk from overdose (Cassidy and Henry, 1987).

Table 12.1 Number of deaths per million prescriptions per year in the UK

Less than 10	10–19	20–39	40 or more
Paroxetine	Clomipramine	Imipramine	Amitriptyline
Fluoxetine	Trazodone	Phenaizine	Dothiepin
Fluvoxamine		Maprotiline	Tranlycypramine
Sertraline			
Lofepramine			
Mianserin			

Psychiatric referral should be considered in the early stages of management if:

- The patient has harmed or is threatening to harm herself. (Urgent Referral.)
- It is proving difficult to determine whether or not the patient is depressed.
- The patient is psychotically depressed, has lost insight into her condition, and has delusions or hallucinations.
- The illness is failing to respond and/or is severe.

Once the doctor has decided to refer the patient, he/she will decide who to refer her to. This may be a counsellor, psychologist, psychiatrist or a community psychiatric nurse. The patient may then be admitted to hospital (this is rare); visited at home by a psychiatrist who will further assess the situation; or placed on the waiting list for outpatient treatment with the professional who has been asked to see her.

Note: Because different members of the Primary Health Care Team will have different skills, and some may have had formal training in counselling or psychotherapy, the GP may refer the patient to them. However, it is important that no counselling be undertaken by anybody who has not been properly trained (and this includes the GP).

Practice nurses

Practice nurses screen for latent diseases such as asthma, diabetes and hypertension. Once the team agrees on the criteria for detection of depressive illness, a screening mechanism can be developed whereby the practice nurse can screen opportunely for depression as part of her health promotion work. One of the tools available is the HAD Scale for the detection of general depression (as opposed to the Edinburgh Postnatal Depression Scale which is only for the detection of postnatal depression).

Depending on how the practice decides to operate, the practice nurse can move beyond simple screening in order to assess the severity of depressive illness. This will require the formation of a protocol among the Primary Health Care Team members, detailing the parameters for the nurse's involvement and the point at which she should refer the patient to the GP. Similarly, it would be useful if the health visitor could also operate within appropriate parameters when identifying and counselling mothers suffering from postnatal depression.

As with chronic illness, the practice nurse can collect information and tag clients' notes to alert the GP.

There are many aspects of the management of ongoing therapy that can benefit from the involvement of the practice nurse. Her key assets are her ability to form and maintain a trusting relationship with the patient and to discuss the management of each depressive episode with more time than is usually available to the GP. Many practice nurses are trained in counselling skills. She can have a key role in assessing the progress of a patient through the use of assessment questionnaires, and through her own personal communication skills. She can then report on progress to the GP and any deterioration can be dealt with by a re-assessment.

The practice nurse can play a vital part in monitoring compliance with medication. She can discuss with the patients how they find taking the medication, and how some of the common side-effects can be minimized. Many people also find it useful to have the reasons for side-effects explained; others benefit from a simple explanation of how the medication works.

Information about social security benefits and a current list of local self-help groups should be available.

Midwives

Midwives are in an extremely good position to pick up problems in the antenatal period and during the time they are visiting after the birth. Because they have often come to know the mother quite well before the birth, they will be quick to pick up any personality changes in the period afterwards. Sometimes the stress that the mother and family are under may lead the midwife to believe that the mother may not cope indefinitely, even if she is all right at the time of transfer into the care of the health visitor. In this case, it is vital that this information is passed on to the health visitor.

Health visitors

The health visitor will find that the EPDS is a valuable tool for recognizing a depressed mother, not least because it acts as an opener for discussion and shows that you are interested in her. When I visit at three months following delivery, I no longer say that I am coming to 'do the weaning visit', although I do incorporate advice about the baby into the visit. I state quite early on in our relationship that at about three months I will be visiting to see how she herself is feeling, and I emphasize that this visit is 'for her'. If she knows right from the beginning that I am interested in her well-being, it helps to put the health-visitor role in perspective. She is more likely to say if problems arise any earlier than the six-week presentation of the first EPDS questionnaire.

Jenni Holden (1988) talks about the need for the health visitor to involve the father in the early stages, discussing with both parents how problems tend to mount up so that the mother feels that she will never be organized again. The husband should be encouraged at this stage to avoid criticism, and to let her know that he still loves her. He should try to protect her from well-meaning advice (such as, 'I saw my mother yesterday and she feels that you are picking the baby up too often'), emphasize his faith in her as a mother and, above all, offer a strong shoulder to cry on. He can encourage her by standing back from the problems, thus making himself more able to help her solve them. If the husband feels that his wife is not coping and life for her is becoming an unsuccessful balancing act between trying to be the ideal mother and reality, he needs to encourage his wife to seek help from the health visitor or GP. Sometimes the father has to contact the health visitor himself because his partner is so immersed in her depression, and he will need a lot of support himself when this is the case.

It is often appropriate to introduce a mother to a recovered mother to enable her to receive peer support; some health visitors maintain lists to facilitate this. They may also give the contact number for a telephone support line (see the list of helpful organizations in Appendix 1). Support groups tend to be difficult to organize due to baby-sitting problems, etc., but if a good one can be set up it can be very useful.

Health visitors must be prepared to give advice on matters other than child care. Non-directive counselling techniques help the mother to feel that the health visitor is interested in her, as well as the baby. Many health visitors are now being trained in the more sophisticated counselling techniques described later in this book (Chapter 16).

Community psychiatric nurses

The community psychiatric nurse (CPN) can still play a key role in the treatment of postnatal depression, if given the structure and the opportunity. Christine Jebali (1991) reported on a research project carried out in the West Midlands which showed some very encouraging results. This small investigation revealed a poor provision of services and a poor appreciation of the mental health needs of women, in particular those with postnatal depression (PND). There were no clear guidelines for joint effort, no clear identification of professional roles, and no clear identification of the skills and competences required to deal with depressed mothers of young children. All too often their problems were trivialized, usually through ignorance. As a result of these findings, a CPN post was introduced in the Wolverhamptom district to work specifically with women suffering from postnatal depression, and in partnership with local health visitors wherever possible. The involvement of the health visitor was though appropriate because:

- It recognized the health needs of the mother as well as the baby.
- It recognized the need to work as a team.
- It encouraged a harmonization of approaches to counselling and improved inter-professional understanding.

Jebali herself found that:

- PND cases had a very low priority and were not well understood.
- Health visitors and CPNs tended to work in isolation.
- Health visitors and CPNs could better coordinate PND services.

The newly provided service for mother and baby attempted to address these findings through promoting a more constructive referral system to maximize input from both CPNs and health visitors. The point was made that, because health visitors are most often involved in the early detection of postnatal depression, it was vital that they were aware that a specialist CPN input was available. To facilitate this, the CPN arranged meetings with many of the district health visitors to convey the importance of prompt, direct referral and the value of close communication and joint working strategies. It was stressed that immediate action can minimize much of the mother's psychological distress. It was decided that the referral system should be flexible and informal so that it would readily encourage the health visitors to contact the CPNs, either to make a referral or to ask advice.

The referral system worked as follows. If the health visitor identified that the mother was experiencing difficulties, with her agreement, she contacted the CPN to discuss the problem. A joint visit was then arranged to enable the CPN to assess the situation and devise an appropriate working strategy together with the health visitor. Communication was then kept clear between the professionals and each knew what the other was doing. Ongoing sessions with the mother were planned, depending upon the perceived needs of the mother and baby. The key worker was either the health visitor or the CPN, depending on the skills needed. This in turn encouraged increased readiness to acknowledge each other's roles and to work together.

Ms Jebali pointed out that the professions complement each other. Health visitors are expert in areas such as sleep patterns, development, immunization and so on, whereas CPNs are the people trained in cognitive and other forms of therapy. Also, many health visitors have, or are in the process of gaining, formal counselling skills. In future many CPNs will not have time for this type of involvement, and other professionals must be ready to take over. However, I do applaud this approach. I hope it may at least be possible for the health visitors to have a key CPN to contact for advice. I also hope that, when a CPN has a special interest in this area, he or she will be encouraged to make a commitment to similar cooperative schemes.

- Find out what the policy is for referral from health visitor to CPN and 'working together' in your area. If there is not one in place, try asking why not.

District nurses

District nurses visit a range of people requiring hands-on nursing care, from a young man recovering from a motor-cycle accident to a woman caring for her elderly confused parent while also looking after a young family. The district nurse may well detect signs of depression in many home situations.

Administrative staff and receptionists

The administrative staff and receptionists need to be aware of the possibility of depression, especially in patients displaying unusual behaviour, and, if concerned, alert the doctor. They should administer the screening procedures decided on by the practice and monitor patient attendance at follow-up visits, gently following up on those who do not attend (although the practice nurse may prefer to do this). They should monitor poster and leaflet displays (and order more as necessary), and develop and maintain a list of useful contact addresses.

REFERENCES

Jebali, C. (1991) 'Working together to support women with postnatal depression', *Health Visitor*, 15: 410–11.

13

STRESS

Based on the guidelines from the NSPCC, and in part linked closely with Chapter 14, the following tips will be useful for both parents. It includes advice to reduce stress within the family when dealing with children of all ages.

THE CRYING BABY

It is important that the new mother realizes that it is normal for a baby to cry. Try the following advice if the crying is becoming a problem.

- Think of the things that your baby may be trying to say. Could it be hunger, a wet nappy, frustration at not being able to reach a toy, or just wanting a cuddle?
- Try rocking your baby in a pram or a cradle, or walking up and down with him or her.
- Try singing to your baby.
- Cuddling your baby is the best tip of all. Make sure you are relaxed – babies can tell if you are tense. Once your baby begins to calm down, don't be too quick to put him back in his cot.
- If your baby seems to cry all the time, ask for further advice from your health visitor or doctor. If it is as simple as something such as colic, much can be done to help these days.

BEDTIME BLUES

It can be very wearing and stressful for a mother who has spent a full day with her baby to find that he or she will just not settle down to sleep. Make sure that her expectations are normal for a child of the age of the one in question and then try the following advice.

- Set a routine to help your child to wind down gradually. Tell him or her that bedtime is coming up but do not make it sound like a threat. Give him or her a warm bath, perhaps followed by a story.
- Ask your partner or an older brother or sister to take over for a while.
- Give up the struggle and let your child play while you sit down and relax before you try again. Remember that children, like adults, vary in the amount of sleep that they need.

Try to see it as a compliment. Small children are often very sad when the day ends because it means that they have to leave the people they love.

THE 'LITTLE MONSTER'

Sometimes a previously delightful child will appear to become a 'monster' almost overnight. This can be devastating for a mother, particularly if friends and family start to comment. Reassure her with the following advice:

- Try to be patient. Children under the age of about three still see themselves as the centre of the world. They don't mean to do anything wrong, and they don't really understand how it makes you feel.
- Distraction is often the best solution. Children soon forget about crying when presented with an exciting object, or if you tell them a funny story or sing a song.

THE 'KNOW-IT-ALL'

Sometimes a mother is coping quite well but will appear to struggle with a newly assertive five- to ten-year-old. Try the following advice:

- If he says something rude or unkind, tell him calmly how he makes you feel, and ask what he is feeling. Don't be tempted to reply with equally unkind comments.
- Try not to have too many rules. Children like to make some decisions on their own.

- You may not like the way your child is behaving at the moment, but it is important to let him know that he is still loved.

THE TEENAGE REBEL

This is a time when parents really begin to tear their hair out and sometimes they also fail to realize that their teenager is also feeling very stressed and pressurized. They still need their parents, yet teenagers often reject them. Nothing mum and dad say or do seems right. They make unreasonable demands, which can end up in a blazing row. It may be appropriate to advise the following:

- Try to discuss any conflicts in a positive way, without getting cross. It is better to 'negotiate' with your child and find a middle way that you can both accept, just as you would with an adult.
- Remember, teenagers are more likely to respect your views if you show respect for theirs. Imposing your opinions may only make matters worse.
- Try not to be too critical. As they become adults, children need a lot of support and encouragement to build up their confidence.

TRYING TO BE SUPERWOMAN

Many mothers feel responsible for everything – their children, cooking, cleaning, shopping and all the other domestic tasks – and perhaps they have a job outside the home as well? Try to encourage mothers not to juggle too many things at once. Ask them to make a list of the essential tasks which can fit comfortably into their day, and suggest that they should just aim to do those tasks.

COPING WITH UNEMPLOYMENT

Unemployment can lead to money worries and a loss of self-confidence, and parents may be tempted to take it out on their children. Suggest that the parents:

- Check with their social security office that they are getting all the benefits that they are entitled to. You can provide help to answer questions and fill in forms, if you think this would be useful.
- Find out from their library or Citizens Advice Bureau whether there are any training schemes, activities or support groups in the area for people looking for work.

Without allowing it to sound patronizing, encourage them to remember that love is the most important thing that they can give their children.

GETTING TO SCHOOL

Trying to make children fit into an adult's timescale can be fraught at times. Offer the following advice:

- Sort out clothes, packed lunches and everything you need the night before.
- Get up earlier than you think you need to.
- Arrange to take turns to do the journey to school, either with your partner or another parent at the same school.

THE WHINER/NAGGER/MOANER

All children, no matter what their age, can drive a parent crazy by constant nagging and whining for something they want. Ask the parent to try the following:

- Distraction can work wonders with younger children. Take them to look in the mirror, produce a surprise toy, or start singing.
- For older children, check out the facts about whatever it is they want. Question your reasons for saying no and stop and think before you make a decision. If you do not feel that it is worth the battle, you could give way. Remember, you do not have to prove 'who's the boss', but to say no first and then constantly give way under pressure can reinforce nagging from the child.

FURTHER TIPS TO HELP THE 'CALMING DOWN' PROCESS!

- Breathe slowly and deeply, and count to ten. Remind yourself that you are the adult, and can set a good example to your child of how to behave.
- Ring your partner or someone you can talk to. The problem may not seem so bad once you have shared it with another adult. This can be the health visitor if necessary.
- Go outside for a breath of fresh air.
- When things really get you down, plan a treat for yourself. Choose something that makes you feel good – a quiet cup of tea, a visit to the shops, your favourite television programme, etc.
- Humour is sometimes the best remedy. Try to see the funny side of things if you can.

STRESS MANAGEMENT

In order to manage stress many people need guidance, and for this reason many people are referred for stress management training. Some practices employ 'sessional' psychologists to come in to advise clients. This cuts down the waiting times for initial appointments and allows a more dynamic team approach to each individual patient. However, there is no reason why the practice nurse or health visitor cannot provide this service for certain patients, particularly when the client has no objections to being counselled by someone she already knows. As for any type of counselling, correct training is essential and guidance should not be offered unless this has taken place. Many Health Care Trusts and Family Practitioner Committees provide short courses in stress counselling, usually in tandem with the Department of Clinical Psychology. The following advice is meant to complement the training but not to replace it.

The first thing to be aware of is the use of stress in our daily lives. There is no doubt that stress is useful if present in the correct amount for optimum performance. It is easy, however, to allow yourself to go into 'overload' after finding that you respond well to only slightly less stress than that which is too much for you to cope with without untoward effects either physical, mental or both.

Generally clinical psychologists use certain response systems to work with patients. The single one, or a combination, they choose will depend on their 'school' of psychology. An overview of all three systems will be useful to allow you a more balanced picture.

KEY POINTS

1. The cognitive system:	Avoiding cognitive distortion Cognitive reappraisal Problem-solving techniques
2. The physiological system:	Exercise Self-health care Relaxation techniques
3. The behavioural system:	Time management strategies Use of assertive behaviour Structuring of leisure time and social activities Addressing personal problems

The cognitive approach to stress management

This concentrates on avoiding cognitive (thoughts and feelings) distortion and helps people to alter misconceptions. For instance, when dealing with a person with relationship problems, it will encourage her to step back and consider whether it is the other person who has the problem. It will also help her to magnify positive areas, and to minimize the more negative areas of herself. She will be discouraged from 'predicting' bad things (for example, 'I am going to have a terrible day today'), and will be taught to think more positively. One of the techniques used is that of cognitive reappraisal. The client is encouraged to compare her problems/situation with others that are 'real' and 'worse', usually resolved ones from the client's own past. For example, if your car breaks down in the middle of the main road while you are on the way to somewhere important and it is pouring with rain, you are likely to start feeling agitated and stressed. If you force your mind to think back to a time when you were in a similar situation but had not renewed your RAC membership, you may feel better as you make your way to the telephone box to summon help!

Problem-solving techniques are important when dealing with the cognitive system, and it is likely that the client will be encouraged to list alternatives and to 'stand back' mentally to consider them.

The physiological approach to stress management

Obviously, this will stress the importance of a good diet, adequate relaxation and recreation and general self-care. As well as keeping the body well, exercise has an important part to play in helping to lift 'low spirits' and/or depression, apart from helping to alleviate stress. This is because during exercise brain chemicals called endorphins are released. These stimulate pleasant, warm feelings of well-being. These chemicals are also stimulated by humour, relaxation, sex and eating favourite foods. This is why people become addicted to chocolate!

The behavioural approach to stress management

This will emphasize the confrontation of certain behaviour and behaviour patterns. For example, if someone has a phobia, it would not be considered necessary to explore the reason for it. It would not matter that a person was terrified of dogs because he/she was bitten by one when he/she was three years old. What would be considered important would be to change that person's behaviour when he/she came into contact with a dog. A more appropriate behaviour would make the person feel better and, if repeated often enough, the behavioural change would enable a more appropriate physiological response to take place each time a dog came on the scene. In other words, it is not important what has caused the problem, but rather how one responds to it. However, this approach is not always appropriate. For example, it would not be the best method of dealing with bereavement and loss, sexual problems and post traumatic stress disorder.

An example of the behavioural approach to managing stress can include *assertiveness training*. To enable a client to become assertive, it may be necessary to direct her to a suitable class. If there is not a suitable class in the area, it may be necessary to set one up, in the same way that you would start a well person, healthy eating or exercise course. The value of group support and encouragement should never be overlooked. I have found it better to plan and teach assertiveness in small groups (which can be divided by three) because this enables reasonably dynamic group work. If you have never attended an assertiveness class yourself, this need not be a problem. With the aid of a good book you can teach yourself as you plan the sessions. For this purpose, and for private reading, I highly recommend *A Woman in Your Own Right – Assertiveness and You* by Anne Dickson (1994). (I must stress, however, that an adult teaching certificate is always invaluable when teaching in a group situation because the use of several different teaching methods will enable you to put over the points in ways that will allow people to learn, while avoiding the boredom issue.)

The content of assertiveness training

Assertion, or assertiveness, involves standing up for your personal rights and expressing your thoughts, feelings and beliefs in an open, honest, direct and appropriate way which does not violate the rights of others. Inability to do this will nearly always lead to stress in the individual concerned. The basic message in assertion is: this is what I feel, this is what I think, and this is how I see the situation. Some people mistake aggression for assertion and for this reason avoid assertion altogether, for fear of being thought to be aggressive, whereas others behave in an aggressive manner because they think that they are being assertive. Obviously, both these approaches are wrong but most of us will slip into one of these roles at some time or other. It becomes a problem when one or other of the roles becomes a way of life.

Assertiveness training helps people to distinguish between aggressive, non-assertive and assertive behaviour.

Aggression involves standing up for personal rights and expressing thoughts in a way which is often inappropriate and always violates the rights of the other person. The usual goal of aggression is domination, forcing the other person to lose, often by humiliating, degrading or belittling them. The basic message of aggression is: 'This is what I feel, your feelings do not count.' The non-verbal behaviours are ones which attempt to dominate the other person. They include eye contact that tries to stare down the other person, a strident voice, a sarcastic tone and aggressive body gestures such as finger pointing.

Non-assertion involves violating one's own rights by failing to express honest feelings, thoughts and beliefs. Consequently, the non-assertive person allows others to violate her; she expresses her thoughts and feelings in such an apologetic, diffident and self-effacing manner that others can easily disregard them. The basis message of non-assertion is: 'I do not count; you can take advantage of me; my feelings do not matter, only yours do; my thoughts are not important, your thoughts are the only ones worth listening to.' The goal of non-assertion is to appease others and to avoid conflict at nearly any cost. Examples of non-verbal non-assertive behaviours are evasive eye contact and nervous gestures. These convey weakness, anxiety and self-effacement, and reduce the impact of what is actually being said. The voice may be overly soft and hesitant.

Assertion involves respect, not deference; the latter is acting in a subservient manner as though the other person is right or better simply because he/she is more experienced or knowledgeable. Two types of respect are involved in assertion:

- Respect for oneself, expressing one's needs and defending one's rights.
- Respect for the other person's needs and rights.

Non-verbal assertive behaviours include firm eye contact (but do not involve staring), body gestures that denote strength rather than aggression, fluent speech and a voice that is appropriately loud for the situation.

Proposed assertive beliefs

The following list of points will create a reliable framework which will encourage individuals to become more assertive and to be true to the ways they really think and feel.

- I am under no obligation to say yes to people simply because they ask a favour of me.
- There is no law which says that other people's opinions are more valid than mine.
- If I say 'no' to someone, and they get angry, this does not mean that I should have said 'yes'.
- I have the right to assert myself even though I may inconvenience others.
- I can still feel good about myself even though someone else is annoyed with me.
- The fact that other people may not be assertive does not mean that the same must apply to me.

- Standing up for myself over small things can be just as important as big things are to others.
- The fact that I say 'no' to someone does not make me a selfish person.
- I have the right to disagree with other people even though they feel just as strongly about their own opinion.
- Just because I have agreed to do something does not mean that I cannot change my mind.
- I have the right to tell others when the way they are behaving is annoying or upsetting me.
- Saying 'no' to a friend is probably not going to make her dislike me forever!
- People I care about may be disappointed when I do not behave in the way they expect, or do the things they want me to do, but this is not a catastrophe.
- If I always have to do things I do not want to, just to get someone to like me, then I have to wonder if their liking me is critical to my well-being.
- Other people do not have the magical ability to know what I want if I do not tell them.
- The fact that other people are inconsiderate and obnoxious can be a pain but there is no law in the universe which says they should not act this way.
- I have the right to enjoy what I am doing and to ask others not to do things which interfere with my enjoyment.
- I may want to please people that I care about, but I do not have to please them all of the time.
- I have a right to express my individuality.

Self-expressions

- Express positive feelings.
- Express negative feelings.
- Express your personal preferences.
- State your point without defensively justifying or explaining yourself.
- Express disagreement.
- State your decisions.
- Clarify your own idea or opinion (this is not the same as justifying or explaining yourself).
- Give information.
- Express concern.

- Offer solutions or suggestions regarding problems.
- Speak positively of yourself (the British find this difficult to do).
- Clarify your intent or motives for doing something.
- Give instructions or assign work.
- State your interpretation of another's actions
- Start and carry on a conversation.
- State a complaint.
- Admit mistakes.

Confrontations

Often a woman may feel under stress when she is unable to protest about the behaviour or attitudes of others. For example she may find the attitude of the health visitor or doctor patronizing or unhelpful. She may feel that she is being labelled as an over-anxious or uncaring mother, or be annoyed that the midwife has not arrived at the arranged time. Other examples include unfairness, overt putdowns, emotional over-reactions, passive or active aggression, rigid silences and 'poor me' helplessness. In circumstances such as these the following advice may be useful:

Confront the other person with his/her behaviour and state how that behaviour has negative consequences for you. Should the person persist in that particular behaviour repeat the negative effect this has on you and voice the positive consequences should the behaviour cease.

Another area of confrontation can be found that involves making or refusing requests. It is a **positive** attitude to be able to request the following: services, specific changes in another's behaviour, information, clarification, assistance. It is a **positive** attitude to be able to refuse requests from others. This may include requests for your time, property, money, thoughts and feelings.

REFERENCES

Dickson, A. (1994) *A Woman in Your Own Right.* London: Quartet.

14

MATERNAL EXHAUSTION

THE DEBILITATING EFFECT OF CRYING BABIES

There is no doubt that the crying baby is the most common problem to be brought to the attention of the GP, the health visitor and the midwife. My own experience of this is extensive, as both my babies cried almost continually. When my first child was about three weeks old I took him to my local health clinic and explained that he cried all the time, that he had been examined by the doctor who could find nothing wrong with him, and that I had been tempted to throw him through the window. The elderly health visitor told me that he probably had colic, which he would no doubt grow out of at about three months. I promptly burst into tears and asked what I could do in the meantime. The conversation that followed went something like this:

> 'Relax, dear. Anxious mothers make anxious babies, and he is not ill after all so you have nothing to worry about.'
> 'But I can't relax, I keep wanting to throw him through the window. I have just got to get some sleep.'
> 'You must sleep when baby sleeps, dear. The housework can wait you know.'
> But he doesn't sleep. He catnaps for ten minutes out of every hour night and day.'
> 'Even so, you must learn to relax because he will cry a lot if you keep carrying on like this. Get someone else to look after him for a few hours and go out and have a break.'
> 'No one will look after him because he cries so much and my husband won't take a turn because he says that the baby hates him. I have told him that, if that is the case, then this baby must hate the whole bloody world.'
> 'No he doesn't, dear. He loves you and you love him don't you?'

'I am too tired to love anyone at present. I am too tired to feel anything and I am telling you that yesterday I wanted to throw him through the window. I have got to get some sleep.'

'In six months' time this will all seem so long ago, and you will wonder why everything seemed so black. Go and see the doctor and ask him if you can have something to help you to relax.'

'I would be able to relax if this sodding baby would let me! Every time I fall asleep he wakes me up again!'

'I am telling you, dear, everything will work out just fine. Just get on with enjoying your baby! Don't waste this precious time.'

'But I wanted to throw him out of the window!'

'Yes, I know, but you didn't did you?'

At this point I left, and I never did attend clinic again. I have never felt so alone in all my life. A couple of weeks later I called out the GP because the baby had a septic finger. He was an older man, Dr Gordon, and we had a conversation in raised voices over my son's frantic screaming. He pointed out that my son had colic. I told him that I knew this but that I was learning to work round the screaming because 'everyone' had said that nothing could be done. The doctor wondered if I had tried picking the baby up and cuddling him? I listlessly explained that there was no point because he constantly kicked away from me when I attempted this. I think that by this time my appearance was verging on that of a zombie, but I had the sense to explain to the doctor that I was rather concerned because I had begun to have peculiar attacks of getting my words all mixed up and experiencing numbness down one side of my body. This rather dour Scotsman gently asked me why I had not sought medical help for my problem with the baby's crying. I explained that another doctor had examined him and told me that he was quite well and that I was not to worry. I added that I did believe that this was colic and I did believe that the baby would grow out of it, but that meanwhile I was so tired that all my hopes and dreams of enjoying this baby seemed to have been drowned in a sea of crying. I asked him if he thought that I might need antidepressants because my own health visitor had mentioned that this might be a good idea. Dr Gordon smiled at me and in the same gentle voice told me that it was not me who needed the medication.

He prescribed some vallergan syrup for 'rat-bag' (this is what I called my son when no one could hear me) and made me promise to contact him again should the problem continue. That night we had a reasonable sleep for the first time in weeks. If you are still alive and reading this Dr Gordon, thank you!

Most women are more fortunate than I was, in that at least they receive some advice on how to resolve their baby's crying problem. The following list includes some of the advice given to a group of women from Leeds in the 1980s (cited in Mary, 1983):

- Moral support.
- 'He'll grow out of it'.
- Leave the baby screaming at the bottom of the garden.
- These sorts of babies are the clever ones.
- Original sin in the baby!
- Leave the radio on.
- Ignore the crying.
- Womb music.
- Dummy.
- 'Can't be colic because the book says it stops at three months'.
- Feed more.
- Stop breastfeeding.
- Change diet.
- Watch mother's diet.
- Give boiled water.
- Stop overfeeding.
- Give solid food at two months.
- Main problem is 'wind'.
- Told child is physically normal.
- Give Phenergan.
- Give Vallergan forte.

Obviously not all this advice was given by health professionals, but this list does give some indication of the conflicting advice given to already tired and anxious mothers. Dr Mary and her team devised the following plan of management to ensure an effective approach. I have adapted it slightly to take into consideration the discontinuation of certain medications and the introduction of medicines such as Infacol.

1. Give time to the mother. Listen to her anxieties.

2. Do not assume that it is a management problem until proved otherwise. Reassure the mother that the baby is not crying because of something she has done wrong.
3. Take a good general history and a history of the crying problem and feeding pattern.
4. Examine the baby and reassure the mother that there is nothing wrong.
5. Ask the mother to keep a diary of events for a week, including crying bouts, measures which did or did not work, and feeding.
6. Sort out feeding and advise a change if you think it is necessary.
7. Organize a home visit by a health visitor to assess the home and family.
8. If colic is involved, try Infacol.
9. If a skin allergy is present, treat it to stop the itching. Involve the GP.
10. If the crying persists, consider whether the baby may be sensitive or allergic to cow's milk. Involve the GP.
11. If crying persists, refer the case to the GP for possible further investigation or use of sedatives.
12. Support the mother regularly. Arrange breaks away from baby.
13. Explore the possibility of setting up a 'Cry-sis' self-help group. The health visitors in Leeds went on to do this.

COLIC

Some babies, suffering from colic, appear to be sensitive to cow's milk formula. Soya formula may be tried for intractable colic but caution needs to be taken because many babies are also sensitive, or allergic, to soya protein. This can also present a problem, for the same reason, when babies are suffering from allergic reactions that are suspected to be connected with dairy products, and are given soya formula to replace it. Other specialist formulas are available and this is why a suspected allergy to cow's milk should always involve the GP who, in severe cases, may also wish to refer the child to a dietitian or a paediatric specialist.

'FUSSY' NEWBORNS

If there is one thing certain in this world, it is that babies do cry. The thing that is not so certain is why, for no apparent reason, some cry so much more than others. They are feeding well, the temperature is right and there is no apparent sign of illness. Usually, mothers will cope quite well during the day but if the child cries at hourly intervals during the night, exhaustion sets in. Often, the problem sorts itself out quite soon and the infant settles into a routine. However, 'soon' can seem forever to a new mother (and father) and I have found the following support strategies useful during the first few weeks.

1. Make sure that the mother knows that she is not doing anything wrong. If she is making mistakes, do not point them out as such. Instead, reinforce the things that she is doing well and suggest a different approach in certain areas.
2. Explain that the only way a baby has to communicate is to cry. This does not necessarily mean that anything is wrong, although possible reasons should always be checked out.
3. If the mother is formula feeding, suggest that she go to bed at 8 p.m. and leave her husband to give the next feed. This will allow her to get at least four hours unbroken sleep and avoid the effects of sleep deprivation. If the mother is breastfeeding, this can still be achieved by the use of expressed breast milk. I make no apologies for this suggestion, as I have often found that this approach actually prevents a mother from giving up breastfeeding altogether. Missing one feed will not cause her milk supply to decrease in the long term. Usually this tactic only needs to be used for two or three nights, allowing the mother to get her second wind.
4. When a baby cries for much of the day the mother will often feel quite hassled about getting the evening meal ready. She will also tend to neglect her own midday meal. Advise her to use easily prepared foods as much as possible. Perhaps her husband can get the tea. If she has a microwave, suggest that she make the meal at a time during the day when the baby is more settled, and then reheat it. Ask her to make sure that the fridge is filled with sandwiches and yoghurts, etc. in the morning, so that she can grab them at a moment's notice. This is particularly important advice for breastfeeding mothers who need all the calories they can get. If finances are a problem,

take this into account and help her to work out how to do it.

5. If she likes to keep her home nice, *do not* tell the mother to forget the housework. This will only make her even more anxious. Instead, help her to prioritize the housework, keeping hygiene in the kitchen and the bathroom to the forefront. Work out what her partner, other children, friends, neighbours can do to help, and then put everything else into perspective with the suggestion that dust is not likely to kill anyone. Try to introduce a sense of humour into the situation while encouraging her to accept that there is a limit to what she can expect to do herself.
6. Encourage parents to take a break away from the baby, even if only for a couple of hours. If the mother is a lone parent, this is even more important.
7. Encourage the mother to stick with one sensible source of advice and not to keep chopping and changing. Also advise her to avoid 'friends' who smugly pronounce 'Well of course, I just didn't have any of these problems. He just went down between feeds like most babies' (the unspoken question being 'What on earth are you doing wrong?').

When I first started health visiting, I realized that advice on sleep management was often quite erratic, ranging from 'leave him to cry' to 'if he sleeps in your bed until he is 15 years old, does this really matter?' Some good books have been written but many mothers cannot afford to buy them, and the local library may be some distance away. I decided to write a pamphlet of my own (see Appendix 3). I hope this will be of help to you.

■ Read my pamphlet on sleep management (Appendix 3). What would you add to it?

REFERENCE

Mary, B.M. (1983) Dissertation to the Leeds Development Paediatric Course. Unpublished.

15

PHYSICAL TREATMENT

Psychological treatment is quite effective in mild or moderate depressive episodes, particularly those with few biological features such as loss of sleep, appetite, weight and libido. Cognitive therapy aims to re-educate people to have more positive views and, in skilled hands, is claimed to lessen the risk of relapse. An excellent report on the developments in the treatment of postnatal depression was published by Professor Malcolm in Lader, 1995.

Patients who are suffering from the physical symptoms of depression will often need physical treatment (drug therapy) as well as some form of psychological approach. With a severely retarded, almost stuporose patient, electro-convulsive therapy (ECT), typically twice a week for up to eight applications, can be very effective.

In this chapter the effects and side effects of different types of treatment are considered. I would like to acknowledge the cooperation of Professor Lader who provided much of the technical information on drug therapy.

MEDICATIONS

The tricyclic antidepressants

Tricyclic antidepressants (TCAs) are still the most widely used antidepressants because their attributes are well known and the majority of them are relatively inexpensive. Most, but not all, are sedative, and are traditionally given as one dose at night to help initiate and sustain sleep and to minimize unwanted effects associated with peak concentrations.

The main side-effects of TCAs are sedation, tremor, constipation, dry mouth and blurring of vision. Postural hypotension and sweating may be troublesome, as may sexual dysfunction, such as delay in ejaculation (Baldwin, 1995a). Weight gain may be marked and resented by the patient; the convulsive threshold is lowered. Alcohol and other central nervous system depressants are potentially hazardous; TCA overdose is notoriously hazardous. In the UK dothiepin and amitriptyline are popular, as is Lofepramine, a newer TCA with fewer anticholinergic side effects and great safety in overdose. (Freemantle *et al.*, 1994). Lofepramine is often useful in treating elderly patients who tend to be particularly sensitive to TCA side effects. The efficacy of TCAs in childhood and adolescent depression is poorly established. (Hasell *et al.*, 1995).

TCA derivatives include mianserin, maprotiline and trazodone. Vilafaxine is another atypical compound derived from propanolol (a beta-blocker). These compounds have differing profiles, but tend to have fewer side effects than the classical TCAs. Venlafaxine is a selective serotonin and noradrenalin re-uptake inhibitor with less affinities for other receptors than the TCAs. In higher dose (up to 200 mg/day) hypertension can occur, so regular monitoring of blood pressure is required. Venlafaxine is favoured by some doctors for treatment-resistant patients but its place in therapy is still being investigated.

The selective serotonin re-uptake inhibitors

Selective serotonin re-uptake inhibitors (SSRIs) have been available for several years. Zimeldine, the first SSRI, was withdrawn because of neurotoxicity. Currently, the SSRIs citalopram, fluoxetine, fluvoxamine, paroxetine and sertraline are available in the UK. They differ somewhat in clinical profile. For example, paroxetine tends to be mildly sedative, whereas fluoxetine is mildly stimulant and citalopram is neutral. All SSRIs can cause anxiety and insomnia, and dosage in some cases may need initially to be conservative. The main side-effects are nausea, vomiting, headaches and sexual dysfunction.

In general, SSRIs are somewhat better tolerated than TCAs (Montgomery *et al.*, 1994), although efficacy is the same (Anderson and Tomenson, 1994). Full dosage is more readily tolerated and, since they are much safer in overdose than TCAs, they are preferred in patients with suicidal thoughts. Rare adverse events include extrapyramidal effects and mild withdrawal syndromes.

Nefazodone combines a weak SSRI action with pronounced

5-HT blockade. It is one of the few antidepressants to normalize sleep patterns, and is associated with a low incidence of sexual dysfunction. It is appropriate for the depressed patient with severe insomnia.

The old mono oxidase inhibitors

These were the first antidepressants to be introduced, and were first marketed in the late 1950s. However, their unclear indications, limited efficacy, side effects of postural hypotension, dry mouth and limb oedema, together with the well-known dangers of potentially fatal dietary and drug interactions, have restricted their use to drugs of third choice, or to desuetude. Moclobemide is a reversible, selective inhibitor of MAO-A with minimal dietary interactions when taken on a full stomach. However, drug interactions with sympathomimetic amines, opioids, etc., remain somewhat hazardous. Moclobemide is licensed for major depression, but is also being evaluated in various phobic disorders.

Antidepressants should be used to treat the appropriate clinical syndrome, that is, major depressive disorder, especially where there are pronounced biological features (Brown and Khan, 1995). Even if the patient's depression is understandable in terms of life events or environment, the depression may still respond to drugs.

All antidepressants seem to be equal in efficacy. Around 70–80 per cent of patients with major depressive disorders respond to full doses. Spontaneous remission and placebo response total about 30 per cent, leaving 50–60 per cent of patients benefiting from antidepressant medication. This benefit diminishes in less typical patients, poor compliers and those with comorbid disorders such as alcoholism or physical illness.

With TCAs and SSRIs, mean response is delayed to about three weeks. Part of this delay is associated with the time taken to reach adequate dosages. With eventual responders, some improvement is apparent at the end of the first week. Improvements in appetite and sleep are particularly noticeable at this time. Conversely, patients who have not responded at all after two weeks on full dosage will probably not respond. The 30 per cent who do not respond may be poor compliers, either because of side effects or misplaced fears of dependence (Lakshman *et al.*,

1995). The remainder constitute treatment refractory depressives, and are commonly referred to outpatient clinics, or inpatient care.

Antidepressants are imperfect medications with useful, but limited, efficacy and various profiles of side effects. Nevertheless, combined with carefully chosen and executed general management stratagems, they can lessen symptomatic distress, morbidity and suicide.

CHOICE OF THERAPY

A good deal of controversy has recently been engendered on this topic. Because SSRIs are much more expensive than the generic TCAs, many budget-restricted GPs are reluctant to prescribe them:

> Some patients tolerate TCAs perfectly well and have responded previously. Others tolerate SSRIs poorly. Both these patient groups can be given a TCA. However, many patients prefer SSRIs, finding them less sedative and with fewer troublesome side effects. Given a TCA, compliance will be poor and response delayed (Lader, 1995).

Professor Lader goes on to suggest that, in his opinion, SSRIs should be the first drug to try on new patients because the lower drop-out rate justifies the extra cost. This is particularly so when the patient is anxious, phobic or has significant suicidal ideation.

There is a trend towards more lifetime treatments (Shae *et al.*, 1992), where antidepressant medication (maintenance therapy) is continued for four to six months after apparent recovery, otherwise relapse is quite likely (Greden, 1993). In the patient who has several depressive episodes, prophylactic treatment is needed to prevent another attack. In the elderly this can constitute 'lifetime' treatment. It is important that the nurse is aware of this because there may be pressure on the patient (from self, friends and relatives) to 'get off those things' as soon as possible. Proper explanation and reassurance need to be given. Compliance is often a problem in antidepressant therapy. It should never be taken for granted that patients will take the prescribed drugs, even though they say nothing to the contrary to the GP. Many times, when counselling a client with recurrent depression, I have been told that she has only taken the drugs for a short while each time because 'I don't want to become addicted'. Although we rightly respect this view, it is important that someone who needs 'lifetime' or long-term treatment understands its prophylactic use, *and also the nature of her own illness*. The patient will often assume that it is weakness, rather than an illness, which makes her feel depressed. She may also think that the antidepressants act by making her feel happy, in a similar way to amphetamines, rather than by righting a biochemical imbalance. I have never found a patient who is not receptive to this explanation, as long as the problems causing the depression are appropriately addressed.

SUICIDE RISK AND ANTIDEPRESSANT TREATMENT

Depressive illness is the most important risk factor for suicide. Therefore, its recognition and its appropriate management are essential if suicide is to be prevented. Usually, when there appears to be a risk of suicide, treatment will include an antidepressant drug. Suicide by overdose of an antidepressant drug has been described as a small factor in the approximately 6,000 suicides in the UK per year, but the figure of 4 per cent (Edwards, 1995) underestimates the real extent of the problem. Seventy per cent of depression is *undiagnosed* and, of the patients who are diagnosed as depressed, *only a minority are prescribed an antidepressant*. It follows, therefore, that the actual risk of suicide in patients prescribed an antidepressant may be *ten times greater* than the crude estimate (Henry *et al.*, 1995). It should also be remembered that when an individual is very depressed she is unlikely to have the motivation to find the means to take her own life. As the medication begins to take effect, the depression begins to lift and she may go through a very crucial stage during which she remains depressed, but feels well enough to be motivated to take her own life.

The potential of antidepressants to cause death by overdose should be carefully considered when prescribing because the likelihood for serious or fatal poisoning differs from drug to drug. Most deaths from antidepressant overdose (over 80 per cent) are due to amitriptyline or dothiepin. (Inman, 1988; Henry *et al.*, 1995). It follows that, although death from overdose of an antidepressant accounts for a small proportion of all suicides, it is responsible for as many as half the suicides in patients prescribed an antidepressant. Many patients cannot tolerate the side effects of TCAs and may confuse them with recurrence of original depression, causing them to take steps to 'end their misery'. The major toxic effect following overdose of a TCA is impaired cardiac conduction due to the blockage of fast sodium channels, leading to cardiac arrhythmias and heart failure.

ANTIDEPRESSANTS AND SLEEP PATTERNS

It is estimated that 90 per cent of depressed patients suffer from sleep disorders (Kupfer *et al.*, 1987). Major depressive disorders are associated with a variety of sleep disturbances that include insomnia, decreased restorative, short-wave sleep, multiple awakenings throughout the night, decreased light sleep and short latency to the first rapid eye movement (REM) period. (REM is the important period of time associated with dreaming.)

Most antidepressants, including TCAs and SSRIs, act as potent REM sleep suppressors and it has been suggested that antidepressant efficacy is linked to REM sleep suppression (Vogel, 1983). SSRIs have also been shown to increase arousals and fragmented sleep above base-line levels in patients with major depressive disorder (Hendricks *et al.*, 1994). The sleep effects of nefazodone, a 5-HT antagonist that also inhibits serotonin uptake, differ from TCAs and SSRIs. Nefazodone improves sleep disturbance in patients with major depressive disorder, decreasing the number of arousals and light stage-one sleep. It also has little effect on REM sleep. The improvement in sleep architecture has been reported in both open trial studies and double-blind comparisons of nefazodone with fluoxetine (Armitage, 1995). The findings also show that the antidepressant efficacy of nefazodone is not tied to REM sleep suppression.

ANTIDEPRESSANTS AND SEXUAL FUNCTION

Psychotropic drugs may have adverse effects on sexual reaction and response. The sexual dysfunction may include reduction of sexual desire, the reduction of physical arousal levels and the loss, delay or alteration of orgasm. Both women and men may be affected in these ways. Within the central nervous system, effects such as sedation may result in a general decrease in the level of sexual interest and activity, and specific effects on neurotransmitters may have a detrimental effect on sexual arousal and function (Baldwin 1995b).

ELECTROCONVULSIVE THERAPY

Electroconvulsive therapy (ECT) is still used with good effect on some *intractable* cases of depression. Although it seems barbaric, the passing of an electric shock through the brain to cause a convulsion is effective and this has been borne out by many studies (for example, Groves and Pennell, 1995). It is most effective on severely depressed patients who display psychomotor retardation. Unlike antidepressants, its effects are immediate. This can be crucial and life-saving for patients whose illness is stopping them from eating or drinking, or is making them wish to take their own life.

ECT has a bad name because of its rather horrific history. Convulsions were first used to treat mental illness in the 1930s under the premise that epilepsy and schizophrenia could not co-exist. This was later shown to be untrue, but ECT still worked and came to be the main treatment for several mental health problems. In the beginning, the treatment was given to patients without the use of an anaesthetic. The patient immediately lost consciousness, and a full convulsion followed. The patients sometimes fractured bones as they thrashed around. Strapping down was found to reduce this problem, but this practice only added to the terror of the unfortunate victim. Before 1959, ECT could be given to patients without their consent.

The giving of ECT has now been reduced considerably and it is only used for four conditions. For us, this is of particular interest because one of the conditions is severe postnatal depression or psychosis. (The others are severe depression with suicidal urges or the inability to eat or drink; depression in those whose physical health makes it inadvisable for them to take antidepressants; and certain kinds of schizophrenia and mania.) The treatment is given by two doctors – an anaesthetist and a psychiatrist – and nurses are in attendance. An electric shock, about one-tenth the strength of that used for restarting the heart after cardiac arrest, is administered. The treatment lasts a minute and from start to finish the procedure is over in about ten minutes.

Some people recover very quickly, but they often have a headache or feel nauseated. Short-term memory is quite commonly affected. This treatment is frequently carried out on an outpatient basis, although the patient must be accompanied home afterwards.

REFERENCES

Anderson, I.M. and Tomason, B.M. (1994) 'The efficacy of selective seratonin uptake inhibitors in depression: a meta-analysis of studies against tri-cyclic antidepressants', *Journal of Psychopharmacology* 8: 238–49.

Armitage, R. (1995) 'Microarchitectural findings in sleep EEG in depression: diagnostic implications', *Biological Psychiatry*, 37: 72–84.

Baldwin, D.S. (1995a) 'Psychotropic drugs and sexual dysfunction', *Reviews in Psychiatry*, 7: 261–73.

Baldwin, D.S. (1995b) Depression and sexual function. Abstract from the Modern Management of Depression Conference, Brussels, April 1995.

Brown, W.A. and Khan, A. (1994) 'Which patients should receive antidepressants?' *CNS Journal: Drugs*, 1: 341–7.

Edwards, J.G. (1995) 'Suicide and antidepressants', *British Medical Journal*, 310: 205–6.

Freemantle, N., House, A., Song, F., Mason, J.M. and Sheldon, T.A. (1994) 'Prescribing selective seratonin reuptake inhibitors as a strategy for the prevention of suicide', *British Medical Journal*, 309: 249–53.

Groves, P. and Pennell, I. (1995) *The Consumer Guide to Mental Health*. London: HarperCollins.

Hasell, P., O'Conell, D., Heathcote, D., Robertson, J. and Henry, D. (1995) 'Efficacy of tricyclic drugs in treating child and adolescent depression: a meta-analysis', *British Medical Journal*, 310: 897–901.

Hendricks, W.A., Roffwarg, H.P., and Grannemann, B.D. (1994) 'The effects of fluoxetine on the polysomnogram of depressed outpatients: a pilot study', *Neuropsychopharmacology*, 10(2): 85–91.

Henry, J.A., Alexander, C. and Sener, E.K. (1995) 'Relative overdose mortality of antidepressants', *British Medical Journal*, 310: 221–4.

Inman, W.H.W. (1988) 'Blood disorders and suicide in patients taking mianserin or amitriptyline', *Lancet*, II: 90–2.

Kupfer, D.J., Foster, G.F., Reid, L., Thompson, K.S. and Weiss, B. (1987) 'EEG sleep changes as predictors in depression', *American Journal of Psychiatry*, 133: 622–6.

Lader, M. (1995) 'Developments in the treatment of depression', *Hospital Pharmacist*, December.

Vogel, G.W. (1983) Evidence for REM sleep deprivation as the mechanism of action of antidepressant drugs, *Neuropsychopharmacol Biological Psychiatry*, 7: 343–9.

16

COUNSELLING

This chapter is based on information from *Counselling: The Skills of Problem Solving* by A. Munroe, B. Manthei and J. Small (London: Routledge, 1989).

WHAT MAKES A GOOD COUNSELLOR?

At the outset it is important to understand the difference between the work of professional counsellors and the work of professional health care staff who use counselling skills.

A professional counsellor undertakes a specific training course, that includes counselling skills and leads to a professional qualification.

Many health professionals will find themselves using counselling skills as a matter of course: for instance a midwife dealing with a mother deserted by her partner in pregnancy; the health visitor helping a mother as she struggles to come to terms with her new role; the practice nurse talking the mother through her child's future asthma treatment. Sometimes a health professional will choose to specialize in counselling either full time or as part of her job, for example the Community Psychiatric Nurse (CPN) and the clinical psychologist. However other health professionals such as the GP, the health visitor and the practice nurse are more and more likely to undergo training in counselling as they use counselling skills in their daily work.

There are many schools of counselling and psychotherapy. The type of counselling practised by community health professionals is often non-directive; this involves reflecting on the problem, formulating it and giving it back to the client. However, many will also use directive methods. These are more challenging and involve more direct questioning.

Counselling is unlikely to succeed if the client does not see the need for it or does not like the counsellor. It is very important that the person doing the initial referral (for example the GP or the health visitor) should explain to the client why counselling will be helpful. The client should not feel that she is going to see a counsellor because she 'has to' or because the referrer thinks she is 'mad' or 'a nuisance'. She also needs to be reassured that she will not be wasting anyone's time. It is very important that, wherever possible, she has the support of her friends and family before the counselling is embarked upon; sometimes it will help if pre-counselling can be given to both partners. Men, in particular, tend to feel threatened or hurt that their partner cannot get better by talking to them, or worried that personal issues are not being 'kept in the family'. The mother may feel disloyal and compound her feelings of low self-worth.

Self-awareness

When a health professional embarks on a course to improve her skills, she will often feel threatened when asked to take part in activities to improve her own self-awareness. These often take the form of group work where the participants get to know each other and themselves, often delving quite deeply. This can cause feelings of intense discomfort until the group has been under way for several sessions.

Why does a counsellor need to develop self-awareness?

We need to find out about ourselves in order to differentiate ourselves from others, so that we can be confident about our own perceived place in the world. We need to develop our sense of 'self' as a thinking, independent individual able to act on our own (be autonomous) and allow ourselves to distinguish between our problems and those of our clients. It is important that we develop a sensitivity to the needs of others and as well the interpersonal skills to do this. At all times we must remain aware enough not to 'get lost' in others' needs. If we attempt to practice the skills we are learning without sufficient self-awareness there is a very real danger that we will appear empty and robotic.

What is self-awareness?

It relates to our perceptions, feelings and thoughts. It encompasses our values, our motivation and the reasons we behave as we do; what causes us stress, and what stress level prevents us from coping. It includes the recognition of our own behaviour and how it impacts on others: what our feelings are towards ourselves, others, and the situations in which we find ourselves. The factors that influence the way we perceive and think about events and the way in which we have perceived events in the past. Our own needs and wishes must be clearly defined whilst understanding how our efforts to fulfil these needs and wishes affect other people. We must also be able to understand how we participate in situations with others.

Once we have come to know and understand ourselves reasonably well, we will use the important skills related to counselling more effectively. For example, empathy is a way of being, not merely a communication skill.

Listening skills

It is important to listen. It helps to create a rapport with the client, and enables the counsellor to find out more about her. Listening well – *visibly* attending – gives the client confidence to express her feelings more openly. Strategies include:

- Facing the client squarely, which says you are available to work with her.
- Adopting an **open** posture which says that you are open to the client and not being defensive.
- Leaning towards the client to show interest and attentiveness.
- Maintaining good eye contact but not staring. The more at ease you are with yourself the more this will be possible. It is important to remember that in some cultures direct eye contact is considered a form of rudeness.
- Remaining relatively relaxed to indicate your own self-confidence. This also helps the client to relax.

Blocks to effective listening

- counsellor's own problems
- counsellor stress and anxiety
- awkward seating arrangements or uncomfortable surroundings

- value judgements and interpretations
- talking too much

Things to remember about listening

Red-flag

To some individuals, certain words can provoke an angry response. When they hear them they become irritated or upset and may stop listening. They tune out the speaker when they begin talking about something which provokes irritation, distress or discomfort in them, for example sexist or racist comments or remarks about working mothers.

'Open ears – closed mind'

Sometimes people decide rather quickly that either the speaker or the subject is boring, that what is said makes no sense or is untrue. They may think that they can predict what is going to be said next and conclude that there is no real reason to listen because they will hear nothing new.

Glassy-eyed

Sometimes we look at a person intently to give the appearance of listening although our minds may be on other things. We drop back into the comfort of our own thoughts, become glassy-eyed and allow a dreamy expression to appear on our faces.

'Too deep for me'

If what we are hearing is too difficult or complex we may 'shut off' and not listen to what is being said.

Being problem centred

Sometimes we concentrate on the problem instead of the person. Detail and fact about the incident become more important than what the person is saying about herself.

'Fact'

Often, as we listen to people, we try to remember the facts and repeat them over and over again to drive them home. As we do this, the speaker has gone on to new facts and we lose them in the process.

A checklist to help you evaluate your listening skills

- Am I reading the client's non-verbal behaviours and noting how they modify what she is saying verbally?

- Am I careful not to over-interpret a facial expression or gesture?
- Am I noticing the mixture of feelings and behaviours that the client is expressing?
- Am I listening carefully to the client's point of view, even when I can sense that this needs to be challenged?
- Do I move beyond empathetic listening, carefully noting whether the client exaggerates, contradicts herself, misinterprets reality, holds things back and so forth?
- Am I aware of my own biases and how they affect my ability to listen?
- What distracts me from listening more carefully? How can I remedy this?

Empathy

To empathize we need to communicate well so that we can enter other people's frames of reference, the ways they interact with the world. It is possible to *be* the other person, but we can construct reasonably correct albeit limited understandings. We need to keep an open mind, be cautious in appraising others, and consider most of our judgements as tentative.

Phrases that are useful when you trust that your perceptions are accurate and the client is receptive include:

You feel . . .
From your point of view . . .
In your experience . . .
It seems to you . . .
From where you stand . . .
As you see it . . .
You think . . .
You believe . . .
What I hear you saying is . . .
I'm picking up that you . . .
You figure . . .
You mean . . .

Phrases that are useful when you are uncertain of your perceptions or it seems that the client may not be receptive:

Could it be that . . .
I wonder if . . .

I'm not sure if I'm with you, but ...
Correct me if I'm wrong, but ...
Is it possible that ...
Does it sound reasonable to you ...
From where I stand you ...
Could this be what is going on ...
This is what I think I hear you saying ...

The use and misuse of questions

Questioning to help a client clarify her meanings and feelings can be very useful but needs to be handled with sensitivity.

Helpful questions

These are usually open-ended and invite further exploration.

Elaboration questions
These are open questions that invite the client to expand on what she has begun to share with you and to explore the issue in greater depth: 'Could you say a little more about that?' 'Is there more you want to tell me about that experience?'

Specific questions
To help the client to deepen her understanding by bringing out further detail: 'You say your youngest child bothers you. Can you say a little more about what makes you feel this way?' 'Can you give me an example?' 'When you say that he is being difficult again, what exactly is he doing at the moment?'

Questions about feelings
These questions can be very useful in depending client insight but you must use your initiative and experience to judge when to be direct, when to be tentative, when to be gentle: 'How do you feel about that?' 'I am wondering what the meaning of all this is for you?'

Unhelpful questions

Remember that too many questions can make the client feel that she is undergoing an interrogation!

Leading questions
Try to avoid questions that imply a particular answer: 'Don't you think you are being a bit hard on your older child?'

Closed questions
Closed questions do not invite further exploration and can create silences that end with the counsellor asking even more questions. They require only a 'yes' or 'no' answer: 'Do you feel angry with him?'

'Why' questions
Avoid 'why?' as far as possible. Very often clients come for counselling in order to discover why something in their life is the way it is. They don't know the answer! 'Why' questions can create defensiveness, can feel threatening, and can create a sense of interrogation.

- Non-verbal communication skills
  - Think back to times in your experience when you have counselled clients, a friend or a member of your family. Do you have a tendency towards any unhelpful methods of questioning? What are they?
  - What would you do if you came up a situation where you could not achieve unconditional, positive regard for your client. Would this affect your ability to empathize with her?
  - In what ways are you self aware?
  - Do you think that your self-awareness could be improved?

Reflection

This is a useful counselling skill best explained by the following examples:

Reflecting content: Restate the client's words in a similar form.
Client: I'm really worried that my baby will be brain damaged by her immunizations.
Therapist: You're worried about your baby's immunizations.

Reflecting feelings: Focus on the client's underlying feelings. Pay attention to non-verbal messages.
Client: The baby is having her first immunizations next week and her brother was really ill afterwards. Of course, she'll still be having it. (Looks and sounds anxious/worried/hesitant.)
Therapist: Yes, Suzy's immunization is due soon and I can see that you are worried that she may have a bad reaction to it.

The therapist has identified the client's worry and anxiety and uses this to elicit more talk about her problems and feelings.

If you are not accustomed to this technique it may be useful to try some role play.

Suggestions for the use of basic empathy

It is important to listen carefully to the client's point of view and to set aside your biases and judgements. Try to walk in your client's shoes. This sounds easy until you come up against a point of view which you strongly disagree with. As the client is speaking, listen to the content of what she says and identify the core messages. Remember that these messages are conveyed both verbally and non-verbally. Always acknowledge each core message briefly (this can be done with a brief 'mm', 'I see' or nod of the head). It is important that you remain flexible enough for the client not to feel 'pinned down' at any point. At the same time as being gentle, it is necessary to keep the client focused on important issues. Move gradually towards exploration of sensitive topics and feelings.

After responding with empathy, listen carefully to cues that either confirm or deny the accuracy of your response. Determine whether your responses are helping the client to remain focused and to develop and clarify important issues. At the same time, note any signs of client stress or resistance. Try to judge whether these signals are conveyed because you are inaccurate or because you are too accurate. At all times try to keep in mind that empathy is a **tool** to help clients see themselves and their problem situations more clearly, and thus to manage them more effectively.

SUPERVISION

Ongoing supervision of counsellors is widely recognized as both desirable and essential to the effectiveness of counselling services. Unfortunately it is a relative new concept to nurses in the community, although psychologists and social workers are generally accustomed to the idea and find ongoing supervision very beneficial.

The general goal of any supervision session is to increase the counsellor's knowledge of themselves and their interaction with others. Supervisors can help counsellors to become aware of their specific competencies and weaknesses, and can then work with counsellors to enhance or remedy them. It may be useful for the supervisor to encourage the counsellor to identify specific problems, generate realistic solutions and implement preferred remedies. It is important that nurses, and other health professionals working in the Primary Health Care Team, demand supervision from trained and qualified counsellors whom the team members respect and trust.

The following list of suggestions for supervisors may be useful to members of the Health Care Team as they co-plan their supervision.

1. Begin by asking the team member what issues she wants to work on, including specific **issues** that she would like the supervisor to listen for and comment on.
2. Ask for sufficient background information about the topic.
3. Ask for a brief, subjective assessment of the case, issue or work situation under discussion.
4. If you are using video or audio recordings play a portion of the tape. Stop the tape at specific points.
5. Focus on actual skills used in counselling and their application to the case in question, including the overall trend.
6. Encourage self evaluation and the expression of doubts or questions.
7. Focus on the overall handling of the case rather than details.
8. Encourage the team member to suggest her own solutions to particular dilemmas.
9. Make sure that you are being helpful.
10. End each supervision session on a constructive note. The team member should have clear goals and the ways to achieve them.

17

A NEW INITIATIVE: A SELF-REPORT SCALE

In March 1996, *Health Visitor* magazine published a report on the development of a self-report scale to be used for depressed mothers. The work to develop this scale was undertaken by Marilyn Hackney, lecturer in psychology and health at Manchester University, and Sylvia Braithwaite and Gillian Radcliffe, nursery nurses at the Stoke-on-Trent parent and baby day unit. I found this research very interesting and I think it could well give other health professionals a lead forward in this area.

As we learned, the quality of the mother–child relationship can account for impairments in the intellectual, emotional and social development of children. Research on mothers suffering from a depressive disorder indicates that this disorder can cause poor quality of mother–infant interaction, which manifests itself in the mother's lack of emotional availability and sensitivity to the child's state (Mills *et al.*, 1985). To assess the quality of these interactions the HOME inventory or rating scale is available (Bradley and Caldwell, 1976). This is based on the study of the mother and child in certain situations and makes judgements based on observations of their relationship. However, it was felt that a self-report, in a similar style to the EPDS, would give a more pertinent idea of how the mother feels about her children. This would be seen as a complementary tool which would be added to clinical observations. It was also anticipated that the use of this new scale would encourage the mother to concentrate on different aspects of her relationship with her child and assist the health professionals in diagnosing and ameliorating potential difficulties.

THE PARENT AND BABY DAY UNIT

Preliminary investigations for the scale were conducted in the parent and baby day unit in Stoke-on-Trent. This is a specialist unit that supports and treats families affected by psychological difficulties related to childbirth. Within the unit, the EPDS is used as a screening tool to help staff make clinical decisions relating to admissions. The Scale may then be used at intervals during the patient's treatment programme. With this in mind, it was felt that a self-report scale would be useful in highlighting any problems in the mother–child relationship,

After discussions with the mothers, and bearing in mind potential interaction difficulties, ten questions were devised and made into a questionnaire. These related to issues of feeding, sleeping, crying, management and play. It was intended that the scale would track the EPDS in that it allows the mother to indicate her feelings on a four-point scale. However, it was decided that she would be asked to relate her answers about her feelings to the previous four-week period, rather than to the previous seven days as with the EPDS.

The pilot questionnaire was given to ten mothers attending the clinic for depression, who were asked to provide feedback on the scale's content and meaning. The scale was then adjusted to accommodate these comments, which were primarily concerned with wording and emphasis. The mothers had no problems in completing the scale and were not unduly perturbed or reluctant to answer the questions.

At the same time, the scale was given to eleven mothers, who were participating in a different research project, to assess its use with mothers who were not suffering from postnatal psychological disturbance. The rationale behind this was based on the assumption that if the control group mothers scored low, this would verify the inclusion of the ten items for clients with depression. A low score indicates a good state of mental health in terms of parent and baby interactions. *Thus, if the mother–child relationship is a contributing factor to maintaining the child's psychological condition, highlighting certain facets of the relationship may be a useful precursor to its amelioration.*

The mean score was 8.8 for the control group and 15 for the 'parent and baby' group, indicating that there were likely to be certain interaction difficulties for the latter group.

The scale was then given to certain mothers in the parent and baby day unit, during their course of treatment. This procedure was initiated and conducted by the two nursery nurses, who used the information from the form to complement their own observations relating to the mother–child relationship. They found that using these two separate approaches allowed them to highlight and address certain facets of the interaction process which might be causing difficulties. Using the scale at later times during the treatment could indicate changes and progress caused by the intervention methods used by the clinical team.

This scale is still in its infancy, but it is an excellent example of the progress that can be made towards better observation, communication and treatment when health professionals work together in developing and introducing new initiatives. I hope that, in a few years' time, this tool and others like it will have become as successful and popular as the Edinburgh Postnatal Depression Scale.

THE TEN-POINT MOTHER–CHILD INTERACTION SCALE

The health professional establishes a relaxed atmosphere and then asks the mother to respond to the following statements in terms of her feelings over the past month. She assesses the responses on a scale of 0–3, with 0 indicating complete agreement.

1. I find playing with my child an easy activity.
2. My child can easily cheer me up.
3. I find looking after my child a strain at times.
4. I know when my child needs me.
5. I can interpret my child's different cries: that is hunger, tiredness and so on.
6. I find my child easy to feed.
7. I find that my child's sleeping habits pose problems.
8. I find it easy to keep my child to a routine.
9. I find that outings with my child cause some difficulty.
10. When I need to go out I feel comfortable leaving my child with someone else.

REFERENCES

Bradley, R.J. and Caldwell, B.M. (1976) 'The relation of infant's home environment to mental test performance', *Child Development*, 47: 1172–4.

Mills, M., Puckering, C., Pound, A. and Cox, A. (1985) 'What is it about depressed mothers that influences their children's functioning?'. In J.A. Stevenson (ed.), *Recent Research in Developmental Psychopathology*. Oxford: Pergamon Press.

CONCLUSION

I am very pleased to have ended this book on the uplifting note of such an excellent initiative. To help the depressed mother and her family, it is necessary that we all keep up to date with new knowledge and that we add to that knowledge with our own ongoing research, projects and initiatives. All professionals must work together to achieve this end.

Many of us find ourselves under threat because of monetary constraints and government policy. If we do not act now to encompass the plight of the depressed mother into our professional mandates, then the opportunity might be lost forever. I hope that I have made it clear that all professionals have a part to play, and it is up to each one of us to identify and exercise that part.

When I began work on this book, I thought that I knew a lot about mothers and depressive disorder. I now realize that I knew nothing compared to the many people who have carried out much of the excellent research featured here. It has become more apparent to me than ever, however, that there has been a great need in the past to gather this information in one place and I sincerely hope that I have, to some degree, achieved this. If, in five years' time, this book has become outdated or has to be rewritten because so many more advances have been made in the area of maternal depression, then I shall have succeeded in my purpose.

APPENDIX 1

RESOURCES AND ORGANIZATIONS

DEFEAT DEPRESSION CAMPAIGN

For information on the following resources please write to:
Royal College of Psychiatrists
(Defeat Depression Campaign)
17 Belgrave Square
London SW1X 8PG

Fact sheet in five languages

Health beliefs and norms may differ considerably among communities and cultures. For instance, expression of mood by somatic symptoms is common in some cultures. There is evidence that feelings of guilt are less common than feelings of shame in patients from the Indian sub-continent. It may well be, therefore, that much depression goes unrecognized, especially if the backgrounds of team members are different from those of the patients.

One of the goals of the Defeat Depression Campaign is to reduce the stigma associated with depression so that when people suspect that they are depressed they will consult their doctor. To help achieve this goal, the campaign produced a fact sheet available in five languages: Chinese, Hindu, Gujarati, Bengali and Punjabi.

Each is written by a mental health professional from that ethnic community. A translation in English is also given. They are available free of charge and may be photocopied. Please send a stamped addressed envelope.

Counselling Depression in Primary Care

This is a teaching package produced for the Defeat Depression Campaign by Linda Gask, Jan Scott and Sally Stanart. It covers the skills and strategies which have been demonstrated to be effective in the psychological treatment of patients with depression. It is aimed at primary care workers: GPs, health visitors, practice nurses and counsellors.

Depression: Lifting the Cloud: An Open Learning Package for Nurses

This training package is aimed primarily at general nurses without mental health qualifications. The video lasts for 30 minutes and looks at the importance of recognizing depression in patients or clients, helping them towards the treatment they need, and explaining that this common and treatable illness does not equate with the client 'going mad'. The video looks at depression in various primary care settings and gives tips on the recognition and appropriate referral of depressed patients. A variety of approaches, including antidepressants and psychological treatment, are discussed. The learning unit is available as a stand-alone teaching package, together with an assessment which nurses can complete and return to earn continuing education points.

OTHER RESOURCES

Video: Postnatal Depression (1993)

Running time: 12 minutes, cost: £50.
Covers the subject of postnatal depression in a practical, sensitive and informative manner. Three mothers discuss their feelings and three professionals give their advice, including advice on the prevention of PND. Also discusses the importance of early detection and treatment. An excellent tool to use during any antenatal class.

CTV
Ridgeway Avenue
Newport
Gwent NP9 5AH

Postnatal Depression Network

This network contains published and unpublished work and acts as a contact point for health professionals interested in PND.

Health Visitors Association
Alexandra House
Oldham Terrace
London W3 6NH
0181 871 2100

The Central School of Counselling and Therapy Ltd
118–120 Charing Cross Road
London WC2 H0JR
0800 243463

ORGANIZATIONS

Consult your public or professional library for local and national addresses.

Association for Postnatal Illness

British Association for Counselling

British Association of Psychotherapists

Cry-sis (support for parents of crying babies or children who do not sleep)

Meet-a-Mum Association (mama)

National Childbirth Trust (NCT)

Samaritans

Twins and Multiple Births Association

APPENDIX 2

RATING SCALES

Simplc, wcll-validated paper and pencil tests can play an important time-saving role in the detection and assessment of depression in primary care settings. Early detection and recognition improve outcome.

The most commonly used scales are:

Beck Depression Inventory (BDI).
Edinburgh Postnatal Depression Scale (EPDS).
General Health Questionnaire (GHQ).
Geriatric Depression Scale (GDS).
Hospital Anxiety and Depression Scale (HAD).

The choice of rating scale really depends upon individual preference and the purpose for which the test is intended. Each has its own particular advantages and disadvantages.

BECK DEPRESSION INVENTORY

The BDI is a list of 21 statements which can be completed by the patient or by an independent rater. This scale is particularly useful for assessing cognitive aspects of depression rather than vegetative symptoms. It can be used to give an indication of the severity of depression, change over time and to measure treatment response. The BDI is described in Beck A.T. *et al.* (1961) 'An inventory for measuring depression'. *Archives of General Psychiatry* 4: 561–71. A copy of the inventory can be obtained from: Dr Beck, Clinical Manager, Psychological Corporation, 24–28 Oval Road, Camden, London NW1 7DX Tel: 0171 267 4466).

EDINBURGH POSTNATAL DEPRESSION SCALE

This 10-item self-report scale has been designed to detect cases of postnatal depression in community settings. It can be completed in about five minutes and has a simple method of scoring. The EPDS has adequate sensitivity and specificity and is sensitive to change in the severity of depression over time. It can be completed in the home or clinical settings and has been shown to be acceptable to women. (See Chapter 10 for a full description.) Contact the Royal College of Psychiatry to obtain copies of the EPDS.

GENERAL HEALTH QUESTIONNAIRE

The purpose of the GHQ is to detect a range of psychiatric disorders. It is not specific for depression. It is suitable for use among adults aged 16–65. The simplest version is the 12-item GHQ-12 although longer versions are available. It can be completed by the patient in a couple of minutes and is very simple to score. Studies have used it as part of health checks or as first stage screening. It can be handed out by the receptionist or nurse and the results – such as blood pressure, peak flow or blood sugar – made available to the doctor at the consultation. The doctor can then ask supplementary questions to refine the diagnosis and instigate management where appropriate. Studies have shown that use of such an instrument can significantly improve detection rates of depression and anxiety. Detailed information on the GHQ is contained in Goldberg, D. and Williams, P. (1988) *A User's Guide to the General Health Questionnaire* Windsor: NFER-Nelson. The publishers can supply copies of the GHQ. Their address is NFER-Nelson Publishing Co. Ltd., Darville House, 2 Oxford Road East, Windsor, Berkshire SL4 1DF.

GERIATRIC DEPRESSION SCALE

The elderly are at high risk of depressive disorders and instruments to aid GPs and other members of the Primary Health Care Team in the detection of depression in this group are to be encouraged. The GDS has been developed specifically for use among the elderly and could be administered, for example, during the over-75 health check. It comprises 30 items requiring a yes/no response. A patient's total score correlates with the severity of their depression. The scale is described by Yesavage, J. and Brink, T.L. (1983) 'Development and screening of a geriatric depression screening scale'. *Journal of Psychiatric Research*, 17(1): 37–49.

HOSPITAL ANXIETY AND DEPRESSION SCALE

This 14-item self-rating scale was originally developed for use in hospital settings to distinguish depression and anxiety from somatic illness. It is a valid measure of severity and can be used to assess change in mental states over time. It is available from NFER-Nelson Publishing Co. Ltd., Darville House, 2 Oxford Road East, Windsor, Berkshire SL4 1DF.

APPENDIX 3

WHAT'S WHAT ON A QUESTION OF SLEEP

Q: Should I expect my baby to sleep through the night, now that he is 6 weeks old?

A: Not really. All babies are different, in the same way as all adults are different from one another. Indeed, quite a few babies wake up for one or more feeds in the night until well beyond 12 weeks. However, all babies can be helped towards more social behaviour if they are given a regular bedtime routine. It may also help if, when he is ready for his day-time nap, you put him in his cot *before* he is asleep but just feeling nice and drowsy. This encourages him to accept sleep as a pleasant part of his day, and to accept sleep more readily at the end of his bedtime routine.

Q: What can I do to establish a bedtime routine?
A: This will vary to fit in with the routine of each particular household. However, it must remain the same each evening. An example may be as follows: Playtime, followed by last feed and cuddle. With an older child this may become tea-time, quiet play, bath and story.

Q: How can the rest of the family join in?
A: As it gets nearer to bedtime it is important that the noise gets less and the atmosphere gets calmer. Ask your family to help you achieve this.

Q: Er – Have you ever met my older children?
A: I know that it can be difficult to keep things calm and quiet when older children are around. It may be worth giving your baby his last feed and cuddle in your (or his) own bedroom and insisting on peace and quiet for this short time. To stop jealousy from brothers and sisters, they can have their cuddle afterwards.

Q: How do I go about settling him after his cuddle?
A: Put the baby in his cot just before he falls asleep. Turn out the light, or leave on the night light, and quietly leave the room.

Some babies respond better if you potter about quietly in the bedroom for the first few nights. This reassures them that they have not 'lost you'. Other babies may find your presence an encouragement to stay awake so it is up to you to work out the best way for you and your baby.

Q: What if all this does not work?
A: Despite all your good intentions and best routine in the world, some babies will still not settle, or will wake up frequently during the night.

Check out the following points:

1. Is he hungry? Is he having enough food during the day? Your health visitor will advise you if you are unsure.
2. Has he got 'wind'? This is not so likely in the case of the older baby who is established on solid food.
3. Is he too hot or too cold? Once again your health visitor will advise you if you feel unsure of the amount of bed covers and clothing a young baby needs.
4. Is he in pain? Teething may cause a disordered sleep pattern but it is not as often responsible for a wakeful baby as parents (and grandparents) tend to think. It is more likely to be the culprit if the baby has previously slept well. Do not take it for granted that teething is the cause for pain. Check with your doctor in case your baby is suffering from pain from some other cause, such as an ear infection.
5. Is he lonely? If everything else has been ruled out he probably is, but the middle of the night is just not the time to complain about it.

Q: Should I leave him to cry?
A: Leaving him to cry for long periods is not a good idea. By the end of half an hour he will be distressed and wide awake and so will you! If you lift him up as soon as he cries he will soon 'catch on' and a bad habit will be formed.

Q: Well, what should I do then? Give him a drink?
A: If your baby is over 6 months old, and feeds normally during the day, he should not need a night feed. Try other comfort methods instead. Go to his cot quietly and do not turn on a bright light. Speak to him soothingly so that he knows that you are there. If he uses a dummy, replace it and rub his back gently. Move out of sight for a few minutes and repeat the whole thing again if the crying is not decreasing.

Eventually your baby will realize that he must stay in his cot, but that you are not far away. You may have to do this for a few nights, and it could be worth your while to take it in turns with your husband, especially if you have returned to work.

Another method, which has proved successful for many families, is the use of a low level tape recorder. This may be playing special 'womb sounds' or just be quiet restful music. Our grandmothers did not sing lullabies for nothing! I also know of more than one baby who has gone to sleep promptly to the sound of a vacuum cleaner or tumble drier. This is because the rhythmical throbbing sound reminds them of the sounds they heard when safe in the uterus.

Q: Why does my baby behave like this?
A: It is important to realize that most people wake up during the night but

usually drop off to sleep again straight away. This is what you are trying to encourage your baby to do. If you pick him up as soon as he cries, or take him downstairs or into your bed, he will think that waking up means getting up, no matter what time of the day or night it is.

Q: Is it all right to pick him up and cuddle him during the day?
A: Yes it is. You will not spoil your baby this way. Love given at this time helps a baby feel secure and eventually less demanding. What you are aiming at is to teach him that he need not cry every time he is left to go to sleep. If he cries because he is lonely during the day go ahead and cuddle him – enjoy your baby and get to know him.

Q: Should I try to stop daytime naps, so that he is more tired in the evenings?
A: No. If a child is more used to fighting sleep during the day he will be an expert at it at night time.

Q: My older child is two years old, and she used to sleep so well. Now we are having dreadful problems with her waking during the night. This started after she had an ear infection two months ago. What can we do to encourage her to sleep properly again?
A: This is a very common problem, even for small children who have previously slept well. The causes are many and may include a previously unsettled period due to holidays, Christmas time, illness, moving house, etc.

To get her back into a sleep routine you must decide on a course of action that you have the strength to stick to. An older child understands rules better as long as they remain the same.

Check for obvious causes such as a wet bed or nightmares. Tuck her up, kiss her goodnight and leave her. If she starts crying return every five minutes until she stops and settles. Do not give her a drink unless she is obviously genuinely thirsty or is ill or too hot. Then just offer water. Waking for a nice drink of milk or fruit juice is fairly common. Water is not nearly so worth waking night after night for!

Q: She does not go to sleep until we do. She usually falls asleep on the settee and then we carry her up to bed. Is this all right?

A: Parents do need time on their own and children generally need more sleep than an adult, so this habit should not be encouraged.

Q: But I go to work and I would hardly even see her if she went to bed at 7 o'clock.

A: It is understandable that you feel like this, but it is wrong to deprive a child of sleep so that you can make up the hours that you have lost with her during the day. Remember that it is the quality of time spent with her that matters, not the quantity. Your undivided attention for a shorter period will mean more to her than several hours spent with a tired, exhausted mother. Try to make up for time at weekends.

Q: How can I break the habit?

A: Set a regular bedtime. Guide her towards it slowly by bringing bedtime forward by half an hour each night. Put her to bed before she falls asleep so that she does not get upset when she wakes up later and finds herself alone.

As with a baby, make time for a bedtime routine. This may include a quiet chat and/or bedtime story. It should not include a playful romp! Tuck her up, kiss her goodnight and leave the darkened room.

Good thick curtains are worth their weight in gold on long summer days, as they often prevent too early waking as well as keeping the light at bay at bedtime. If it is not possible to change existing curtains, put up an old blanket to help block out the light.

For children who are frightened of the dark, use a night light or leave the landing light on.

Q: What if she keeps on crying?
A: Be firm and confident. Once again, this is the time to return to the room at 5 minute intervals, speaking calmly and telling her that it is time for sleep now. Do not show anger as this will wake her up more or, worse still, frighten her.

If she is very frightened of being left alone, let her know that you are close by in the next room and let her hear you moving around. Gradually her confidence will increase and this should no longer be necessary.

Q: What if she keeps getting out of bed?
A: Then just keep taking her back! After a few nights she will tire of this and you will find that a few determined hours will have been well spent.

Q: Wouldn't it be easier to let her come into our bed?
A: Think carefully about this and discuss it

with your partner. If you allow a small child to come into your bed, be prepared for the habit to go on for a very long time. If you are happy about this – go ahead!

Some families are quite satisfied with this arrangement, and when your child reaches the age of four or five or so she will want her own space in her own bed again. However, I must say that many families are far from happy with this situation and wish that they had never started it!

Q: My sister had a lot of trouble with her baby's sleeping habits and her doctor gave her some medicine for her. Should I ask for some or was she wrong doing this?

A: Sometimes, when all else fails, your doctor may suggest this. It should be given for a short period as advised by your doctor. It is used to try to get your child into a regular sleeping pattern. It would probably be best to use it together with some of the methods that I have already suggested.

As a general rule, it is better to avoid medicines unless they are really necessary. However, your sister should not feel guilty if she had tried everything else and had discussed the situation with her health visitor and doctor.

Q: Could my health visitor have helped?

A: Your health visitor is always willing to discuss problems such as these with you. If the ideas in this leaflet do not work for you, contact her … she may have some more!

INDEX

administrative staff 128
aggression 136
anorexia nervosa 22, 23–5
antenatal clinics 105
antidepressants 121, 148–9
  ECT 152
  mono oxidase inhibitors 148
  relative risk from overdose 123
  sexual function 151
  sleep patterns 151
  suicide risk 150–1
  tricyclic 146–7
assertiveness training 135–8

babies *see under* children
Beck Depression Inventory (BDI) 171
biological theory 14–15, 20–1
Blackburn study (1991) 60–1
'the blues' 65–6, 104, 105
body language 120
British Journal of Psychiatry 8
bulimia nervosa 22, 26–8

'calming down' process 133
children
  bedtime blues 129–30
  crying baby 129, 140–5
  'fussy' newborns 143–5
  getting to school 132
  the 'know-it-all' 130–1
  the 'little monster' 130
  mother-child relationship 76–9, 163–5
  sleep management 145, 174–81
  teenage rebel 131
  whiner/nagger/moaner 132
clinical psychologist 134, 154
cognitive theory 13, 20
cognitive therapy 146
colic 143

communication skills 119–21
community psychiatric nurse (CPN) 3, 119, 123, 154
  relationship with the health visitor 126–7, 128
confiding relationships, lack of 104–5
conflicting advice 90–92, 142
counselling 121, 123, 124, 126, 133, 154–62
  empathy 158–9, 161
  listening skills 156–8
  non-verbal communication skills 160
  reflection 160–1
  self-awareness 155–6
  supervision 161–2
  teaching package 169
  the use and misuse of questions 159–60

Defeat Depression Campaign 1, 168–9
delusions 9, 123
depressive illness
  causes 11–19
  classifications 8–11
  defined 7
Dexamethazone Suppression Test 14
diet
  depression 61–2
  low income families 58–61, 62
district nurse 119, 128
doctor *see* general practitioner (GP)
drug therapy *see* medications
dysthymia 10

eating disorders 22–8
Edinburgh Postnatal Depression Scale (EPDS) 64, 105, 106–13, 117, 118, 119, 122, 124, 125, 163, 164, 165, 172

electro-convulsive therapy
(ECT) 69, 146, 152
endogenous depression 9–10
exogenous depression 8–9

Family Practitioner Committees 133
feeding the baby
crying babies 142, 143, 144
difficulties 104
self-image 83, 89
follicle-stimulating hormone
(FSH) 71

General Health Questionnaire
(GHQ) 172
general practice 2–5
general practitioner (GP)
conflicting advice 90–92
counselling 154
the crying baby 140, 143
detection and management of
depression 119, 121
EPDS 107, 113
missing depression 2–3, 115–16, 118
practice nurse 124
suicide assessment 122–3
Geriatric Depression Scale
(GDS) 172–3
gonadotrophin hormone 71
grief 8–9

hallucinations 9, 123
Health Care Trusts 133
health visitor
counselling 126, 128, 133, 154
the crying baby 140
detection and management of
depression 119, 125–6
EPDS 107, 109, 110–12, 113
missing depression 116–18
postnatal care 88–9, 90
raising public awareness 119
relationship with the CPN 126–7,
128
Health Visitors Association
(HVA) 95
Holmes Rahe Life Stress
Inventory 29
HOME inventory/rating scale 163
hormonal upheaval (in postnatal
depression) 71–3
Hospital Anxiety and Depression Scale
(HADS) 105–6, 122, 124, 173
human chorionic gonadotrophin 72
human chorionic thyrotrophin 72
human molar thyrotrophin 72
human placental lactogen 72
hypothalamus 71

intermittent depression 10

'learned helplessness' hypothesis 48
learned reinforcement theory 13–14,
20
lone mothers 56–61
luteinizing hormone (LH) 71

major depression 10
maternal exhaustion 74–5, 140–5
medications 121, 123, 124–5, 146–9
choice of therapy 149–50
mono oxidase inhibitors 148
selective serotonin re-uptake
inhibitors 147–8
tricyclic antidepressants 146–7
men
depression in 1
postnatal depression 95–102
supportive fathers 125–6
mental health nurses 3–4
midwife 119, 125
counselling 154
the crying baby 140
detection and management of
depression 119, 125
missing depression 116
postnatal care 83, 86, 88, 90
minor depression 10
missing depression 115–18
mono oxidase inhibitors 148
mood, diurnal variation of 10
mother-child relationship 76–9, 163–5
motherhood, satisfaction with 81, 82,
83

National Childbirth Trust (NCT) 95
non-assertion 33–6, 137
nurses *see* community psychiatric nurse
(CPN); district nurse; health
visitor; midwife; practice nurse

oestrogen 76, 77
organizations 170
Otago Women's Health Survey of Childhood Sexual Abuse 52

panic attacks 36–41
postnatal care 81–9
postnatal clinics 105
Postnatal Depression Network 170
postnatal depressive disorders 64–75
postnatal ward
  care 83, 85, 92–3
  identification of vulnerability to depression 103–5
poverty
  and depression 55–6
  and diet 62
practice nurse 128
  counselling 133, 154
  detection and management of depression 119, 124–5
premenstrual syndrome (PMS) 41–6
primary health care team (PHCT) 3, 4, 5, 37, 119, 121, 124, 162
  recognition of depression 105, 107
progesterone 71–2, 73
prolactin 72, 73–4
psychiatric referral 121, 123–4
psychoanalytical theory 11–13, 19–20
psychologist 123, 133, 161
  clinical 134, 154
psychotherapy 124, 154
puerperal psychosis 66–9

rapid eye movement (REM) sleep 75, 151
rating scales 171–3, *see also* under individual scales
reactive depression 9, 10
receptionist 119, 128
recurrent brief depression 10–11
Rowntree Foundation (Dowler and Calvert report) 56, 60

screening 124, 128
selective serotonin reuptake inhibitors (SSRIs) 28, 147–8, 149, 151
self-esteem 24, 48–54
self-image 83, 89, 90
self-report scale 163–5
serotonin 28, 147
sexual abuse 27, 52–3
sexual function, antidepressants and 151
sleep
  antidepressants and sleep patterns 151
  lack of sleep in hospital 92–3
  sleep management 145, 174–81
social status hypothesis 48
social workers 161
Stoke-on-Trent parent and baby unit 163, 164–5
stress 28–33, 129–39
  categories 28
  cognitive distortions 32–3
  effects 31
  non-assertion 33–6
  postnatal care 82
  signs and symptoms 31–2
stress management 133–9
suicide
  assessment 122–3
  risk and antidepressant treatment 150–1
support groups 125, 126, 132, 135–6, 143

teenagers 131
trait anxiety 81, 82, 83
tricyclic antidepressants (TCA) 146–51

unemployment 131–2

vitamins 61–2
vulnerability to depression 103–13

well-woman clinics 105
work
  mental health 55
  occupation and stress 30–31
  stressors 30

LIBRARY
PEMBURY HOSPITAL
01892 823535